Praise for *Choice Not Chance*

"In *Choice Not Chance*, Coach McCallie passes on lessons she has learned for winning on the basketball court and in life. In this entertaining story, she endorses the ideals of self-determination and eschewing emotions that are as old as the ancient Greeks."

—Allan H. Friedman, MD
The Guy L. Odom Professor of Neurological Surgery;
Neurosurgeon-in-Chief, Duke University Medical Center;
Deputy Director, The Preston Robert Tisch Brain Tumor
Center at Duke

"Choice Not Chance tells the story of a heartfelt and fascinating journey. Joanne P. McCallie's infectious enthusiasm for sports and life will inspire readers of all ages."

—Susan M. Collins
U.S. Senator (Maine)

"Joanne knows how to successfully empower young women to make good choices both on and off the court. Her life is a stellar example for anyone who wants to learn about making good choices on a daily basis, rather than letting chance dictate the course of our lives."

—Clarence Underwood
Michigan State University Athletic Director (1999–2002)

CHOICE *not* CHANCE

CHOICE *not* CHANCE

RULES FOR BUILDING A FIERCE COMPETITOR

JOANNE P. McCALLIE

with Rob Rains

WILEY

John Wiley & Sons, Inc.

Published by John Wiley & Sons, Inc., Hoboken, New Jersey.
Published simultaneously in Canada.

For general information on our other products and services or for technical support, please contact our Customer Care Department within the United States at (800) 762-2974, outside the United States at (317) 572-3993 or fax (317) 572-4002.

Wiley publishes in a variety of print and electronic formats and by print-on-demand. Some material included with standard print versions of this book may not be included in e-books or in print-on-demand. If this book refers to media such as a CD or DVD that is not included in the version you purchased, you may download this material at http://booksupport.wiley.com. For more information about Wiley products, visit www.wiley.com.

Library of Congress Cataloging-in-Publication Data:

McCallie, Joanne P., 1965-
    Choice not chance : rules for building a fierce competitor / Joanne P. McCallie.
      p. cm.
    ISBN: 978-1-118-08711-4 (hardback)
    ISBN: 978-1-118-22349-9 (ebk)
    ISBN: 978-1-118-23120-3 (ebk)
    ISBN: 978-1-118-23122-7 (ebk)
        1. McCallie, Joanne P., 1965- 2. Coaches (Athletics)—United States—Biography.
    3. Women coaches (Athletics)—United States—Biography.   4. Coaching (Athletics)—
    United States.   5. Competition—United States.   I. Title.
    GV697.M367A3 2012
    796.092—dc23
    [B]
                                                                              2011039259

Printed in the United States of America
10 9 8 7 6 5 4 3 2 1

*To Maddie and Jack
and to each and every player*

CONTENTS

FOREWORD   MIKE KRZYZEWSKI   xiii

PREFACE   xv

Introduction   1

Chapter 1   Be Ready for Change and Adventure   9
            Opportunity Knocks   10
            My First Meeting with Coach K   13

Chapter 2   Creating "Choice Not Chance"   17
            We Are All Products of the Choices We Make   18

Chapter 3   The Underdog, Fighter Mentality   23
            A Navy Brat Grows Up   24
            Wherever They Live, Kids Need to Be Motivated   26
            Role Models Help Me Develop My Skills   27
            Nurturing Interest and a Desire to Improve   31
            Graduation Approaches   34

Chapter 4   Nobody Likes Whiners   39
            Arriving at Northwestern and Fighting for
              Playing Time   40
            A Coaching Change   42
            My First (Bittersweet) Taste of the
              NCAA Tournament   46

Chapter 5   Money Alone Won't Make You Happy   51
            What Am I Going to Do with My Life?   52
            Following a Passion: My Return to Basketball   54

Chapter 6   Never Be Afraid to Try Something
             and Make a Mistake   59
             Making a Commitment and Sticking with It   60
             Things Begin to Make Sense   63
             A Nearly Fatal Mistake   67

Chapter 7   Seek Out Mentors: There Is No
             Substitute for Experience   73
             Why the Scoreboard Is Irrelevant:
                Play the Game to Attack and Compete   74
             Learning from Failure   77
             Seek Out the Wisdom of Others   83

Chapter 8   Not All of Your Players (or Employees)
             Will Get Along with Each Other   93
             The Other Side of Success   94
             Learning Balance, Restoring Energy   97
             Expectations for the Future   99

Chapter 9   Life Is More than the Game   107
             Away from the Court, My Priorities Change   108
             Team in Transition   109
             New Developments on the Court and in My Life   113

Chapter 10   Set High Team Goals While Motivating on
             an Individual Level: No Two Players
             (Just Like No Two Employees)
             Are Exactly Alike   123
             Arriving at Michigan State   124
             Lessons from Tom Izzo and Lonny Rosen   126
             Motivating a New Team   129
             Managing Conflict   133

Chapter 11   Everybody Has to Be Challenged to
             See How Good They Can Become   139
             Challenges and Progress at Michigan State   140
             Always Measure Your Accomplishments   143

CONTENTS

Chapter 12   Step Back and Reassess Your Priorities   147
How Can We Improve? What Can We Do Better?   148
Refusing to Give Up, No Matter the Opponent   150

Chapter 13   A Message from Coach Smith
and Coach Wooden   159
*Winning Isn't Always about Who Has
the Best or Most Talented Players*   160
Coming Close Creates Added Motivation   163

Chapter 14   Coach K Teaches, "Do What You
Came Here to Do"   167
Moving On   168
Meeting Another Challenge   174
Getting to Work at Duke   175
*Coach K Gives Me the Message
I Need When I Need It*   179
My First Big Win at Duke   180
Transition at Work and at Home   182

Chapter 15   You Have to Seek Out the
Changes—and See How You Need
to React to Them—to Make the
Team (and Your World) Better   187

Chapter 16   Recruiting Is a True Test of Will,
Discipline, Character, and
Evaluation Ability   197
Getting the Right Group of Players   198

Chapter 17   Competitive Cauldron   207

ACKNOWLEDGMENTS   219
*University of Maine and Michigan
State University*   220
Duke University   221

INDEX   223

FOREWORD

One of the abilities that a good coach at any level and in any sport has to have is the ability to read people. I have always found that the best way to do that is to always look people in the eye.

The eyes reveal a lot about a person's character. The first time I met Joanne P. McCallie, I could see in her eyes the passion and desire she had to coach women's basketball at Duke.

Joanne took a great risk by coming down to interview for the job at Duke before she was offered the position. She was aware of the conflicts that might arise as a result of the interview, but she thought the possible outcome of getting the chance to coach at Duke was worth it.

You could see in her eyes that she had a love for Duke and was honored by the chance to coach here. She "got it" immediately.

One of the things I love about Joanne is her energy. She's very competitive, and she allows those around her to not only support her, but also to make her better.

Joanne has all of the characteristics of being a great leader. She always displays a strong face and mood. She conveys confidence and courage under pressure. In the heat of a game, players feed off of this strength.

The title of this book is *Choice Not Chance*, and I have always believed that the power we have to make choices, and not mere chance, is the primary determinant of future outcomes. It takes courage to decide, "This is the direction we're going." You come to that decision by seeking great advice and support along the way.

Advice is what this book is all about. Joanne has used her experiences to talk about the many times "choice, not chance" has played a role in her life and how others can benefit from her experiences.

Joanne has had great success coaching the women's basketball teams at Maine, Michigan State, and now at Duke, and this book allows her to share her strategies with others.

Part of the motivation behind this book is Joanne's desire to help others. Coaches love to motivate, and here Joanne uses the experiences of her life and career to motivate others, in sport and beyond, to be better through the power of the choices they make.

—**Mike Krzyzewski**
Head Coach, Duke University
and USA National Team (2006–2012)

PREFACE

My life has primarily been about two things: *my family*, which con- sists of my husband, John, and our two children, Maddie and Jack, and my profession, which is coaching women's college basketball.

Trying to live a life of balance and success has never been easy. There have been many highs and lows. It's not a steady thing; it's more like a seesaw. One side has more weight while the other rises, then a push comes and it reverses. It keeps moving, and in that constant movement comes the balance over time.

My professional world and private world often collide, and the push and pull can be both painful and poetic. An instance of this happened to me not that long ago.

One of the most emotional moments of my coaching career thus far took place during the regional finals of the NCAA Tournament in 2011 in Philadelphia. Our team had been trounced, bringing a pain- ful end to a very special season. I was fortunate to work with a very unique and talented team, led by three seniors whom I had enjoyed coaching for four years. I had to face the media at the end of the game—their glaring cameras and piercing questions.

Our 11-year-old son, Jack, showed me the strength of charac- ter that he possesses, well beyond his years, and allowed me to get through this very challenging moment with a smile in my heart.

Moments after the game, I saw Jack, Maddie, and John in the hall- way outside the room for the postgame press conference. The room was as packed as any I had ever seen following a game. Trying to give me some space, John said to Jack, "Let's wait here," meaning outside the media room. Though John tried to stop him, Jack said adamantly, "Dad, I'm going in there." He not only came into the crowded room, but he stood right at the edge of the stairs where I went up on the stage to face the media's questions.

When I got to the edge of the stage after the press conference was over, Jack was waiting for me. I came down the stairs, and he had his hand up to give me a high five. As we slapped hands, he said, "Great job, Mom." I couldn't believe it. The kid is unflappable, and he understands what was going on. He had truly separated himself from the moment, and took me with him as he insisted on standing tall.

I am proud to call myself a Title IX baby, as the barrier-breaking legislation for gender equity in sports was passed when I was a young girl. When John's mother went to college in the 1930s, she played basketball and tennis; however, her teams played only intramural sports (i.e., within the campus) and not against other schools. I found myself in new territory when my own college career began, and many choices presented themselves to girls and women across the country. The question before us was a critical one: How do we face these choices and build our lives and strong programs at the same time?

That is the question I aim to tackle and the topic upon which I focus in this book. I want my experiences to be a lesson for anyone who reads it—anyone who is trying to be successful in his or her job and life, as a parent, coach, mentor, or child.

"Choice, Not Chance" was the theme I started teaching at my first basketball camp. It provided a way for the girls and boys who attended to think about and rise above being victims of circumstance and frustration in their lives. We taught these young people that they could make choices every day—choices that would give them control, even if those choices were small ones, like keeping their rooms clean. From the time, as a teenager, when I chose to practice four hours a day in my driveway (shooting, jumping, dribbling—at first just giving myself something to do, then realizing that it was indeed a passion), basketball has been the choice I made. And it has been one that has richly blessed my life.

There was another choice I made on August 18, 1991, in my hometown of Brunswick, Maine—and that was to wed John. My wedding proved to me that love really is, as I had always hoped, a response to one's deepest values and an affirmation of life. I don't understand why people have jitters at weddings; it was a very natural event for me. In fact, I was the most relaxed I've probably ever been about anything in my life.

I rode in a horse and carriage with my father right through the middle of town on my wedding day, and people came out and waved. It was so much fun to welcome all in Brunswick to our celebration. To me, this event was the product of having countless people who had cared for me and who came to share this special time. I really didn't care what I wore; my mother and sister picked out the dress without me and it fit fine.

We had a rehearsal dinner at the Log Cabin, a restaurant on Bailey Island overlooking the Atlantic Ocean. It was warm, comfortable, friendly, and cozy, and we could look out the window right at the beautiful Maine coastline. We had everything and everybody we needed and wanted there. And years later, the people who were present still continue to provide love and support throughout our marriage.

John and I met at Auburn University in the summer of 1989. I was an assistant coach to Joe Ciampi, and John was working on his PhD in economics. I must admit I was a little uncertain about him at first. This guy kept showing up at different places and even looked in the window once when I was taking one of my MBA classes. I thought to myself (somewhat kiddingly, somewhat seriously) that he might be stalking me. But I soon learned that John was a very interesting guy, with a great sense of life and adventure. We were engaged for almost two years, and we spent that time getting to know each other's families, discussing our lives, and seeing how we worked together. We read books together and talked about them. We spent time discovering our values, challenging each other to find our common ground, and dreaming about our future together.

The births of both of our children are incredible memories. They both took place in Maine while I was coaching there—Madeline Clark McCallie in 1994 and John Wyatt McCallie in 2000. Their middle names are the maiden names of each of our mothers. We both have wonderful, smart, and dedicated moms who provided powerful role models for women in our families, and we wanted to acknowledge their importance in our lives.

My mother is British. She married my dad, a Navy pilot, and came to his country, making it her own. Though she never finished college, she is doubtlessly one of the smartest women I know. She is the one who taught me about the power of choices. Not only did she choose to live in a country not her own, but she made the difficult choice to move her three children from Florida back to Maine, even though it was a long way from her husband's job, all because she thought it was a much better place to raise her family. These brave choices of hers shaped my life; without them, I would not be who—or where—I am today.

I sometimes see nowadays, particularly in young people, that people are driven by their emotions to the point of nonproductivity. Today's world of emotions, combined with split-second communication and technology, often drive careless decisions that occasionally have disastrous results.

I tend to consider and approach life's decisions differently. I call it "right thinking," a phrase I use with my team, and it refers to the idea that we are going to be reasonable and allow reason to drive our emotion. The essence of "right thinking" is truly the notion that we are going to *make choices*. We are going to approach the situation, whatever it may be, in a clear, thought-out, and passionate way that extends to how we think and act. I want to use my experience to educate others about the importance of the decisions they make and how those choices affect their future and those around them. Thinking deeply, feeling deeply, and making choices are all part of a philosophy that guides both my life and my coaching. "Choice Not Chance" is a way to live and to think—both as individuals and as a team.

I have been fortunate to coach the women's basketball teams at Maine, Michigan State, and Duke for the past 20 years. Maine was my home state, and it was a joy to start my career there. Michigan State offered me an opportunity to work in the Big Ten Conference with a great group of women who drove us to the National Championship game in 2005—an unforgettable experience.

Being recruited by Duke echoed an earlier choice in my life. After I was named a *Parade* magazine all-American high school player, several college choices were available to me. A woman named Jacki Silar from Duke called, and I went to visit the school. Not only was it a beautiful campus (especially to a girl from frosty Maine!), but the basketball program was strong, and therefore attractive to me. Unfortunately, my mother could not go with me on this trip, and her absence gave her less information about Duke when it came time for us to discuss as a family where I was going to go to school. I accepted an offer from Northwestern and have never regretted it.

So, when the second call from Duke came, this time with an offer to become the head women's basketball coach, it harkened back to the earlier call that I had passed up. You don't get many second chances in life, and this time I said yes, accepting the offer to become the head coach.

Little did I know that by making this choice I was entering uncharted territory, both for myself and for women at large. Usually, women, and many coaches overall, stay at the schools where they take a job as a head coach, making a career of the program they build. My situation differs somewhat; I have been the head coach for three different schools that were part of four different conferences. The pressures of building up a program are enormous. Having done this while simultaneously giving birth to and raising two children—in addition to nurturing a strong marriage and family life—has been an amazing experience. My commitment to both areas of my life has required sacrifices on both ends. I have ached when I have had to miss my own children's activities or games, and I have cut short or found substitutes for work when family duties called. The seesaw that I mentioned before kept moving with the pulls and pushes of balancing family and work.

I felt self-doubt arise many times; it simply couldn't be helped. Though you can be a fighter when the challenge is present, the time comes when doubt rises gracefully on its own. This is when you seek renewal and need a team of people to help you through. You must also figure out how to clear and fortify your energy. One day I walked into the acupuncturist's office and just cried. And although it can help to sit in a room for a while, you have to get back out there. You need people to lean on—people other than your family to act as a support system. I have found that older women and other practitioners are role models, and that sometimes just a conversation with one of these individuals is enough to keep me going. You have to ask for help, make the connection, and be in touch with your emotion to let it out. I call this "clearing"—clearing your emotions and finding a method to renew yourself and tip the balance back in your favor.

Making choices, seeking balance, and restoring energy are all part of a process that becomes a way of life, a philosophy, a way to think as a competitor, as a mother, coach, mentor, wife, or friend.

Writing this book has not only been a way to clear and restore my energy, but it has been a fulfillment of a promise I made to my daughter years ago. When we were in Maine and Maddie was only four years old, we went one day to ride her favorite horse. Even then, my time had been divided between family and work, and I felt pressures about which Maddie knew nothing. She only wanted to be with her mother and spend time playing. We were laughing at the pony, and I half joked to Maddie that one day, by the time she graduated from high school, I would write a book to explain the moments of being born into a coaching family and having a mom who also was a head coach.

The time has come. Maddie graduates in June 2012. She has lived within these stories and has suffered the ups and downs of our life together. For these reasons, I chose to start this book with a letter to my daughter.

Coach P. talking to her son, Jack, on press row at Cameron Indoor Stadium during the 2009 Duke Women's Basketball Blue and White Scrimmage on October 25, 2009.
Source: Duke Photography

INTRODUCTION

My dear Maddie,
Soon, you will graduate from high school and move on to college, becoming even more independent and going forward with your life.

Your father and I have been blessed to have you and your brother Jack in our lives, and before you graduate, I want to fulfill a promise that I made to you a long time ago. When you were about four years old and we were living in Maine, we would escape to the barn frequently to ride our horse, Fancy Face. We talked as a mom and daughter, and I said to you in a very carefree way one day, "Oh, Maddie, someday I'm going to explain all this to you and write you a book about Mommy being a coach and all." That's where the idea for this book started, before your brother Jack was even born.

Yet this is not just any ordinary book. My goal in writing this is to help provide you with a more complete understanding of our lives together, and to help you become a better person by learning through my experiences. Like every working mother's, my life has been filled with difficult challenges—and remarkable moments. I have been thrilled to be a wife, a mother, and a college basketball coach. All of those experiences have provided me with knowledge that I truly want to pass along to you.

Sometimes there are not enough hours in the day to do everything that needs to be done, and that is a frustrating feeling. I have always viewed this balance as a continuous journey—sometimes all-consuming and sometimes overwhelming—but certainly always powerful beyond measure.

You have been there for a lot of the great times we have shared as a family, the joy of big victories and the celebrations that followed. Luckily, there have not been too many low moments; but like every family, we have endured those together as well.

You don't remember how I went back to work when I was coaching at the University of Maine immediately after you were born. I probably should have stayed home longer with you. However, I loved my job, and as a young coach I was very eager to get back to a special team and show them that I could be both a good coach *and* a good mom. It was a couple of years later when the exhaustion finally hit me, and I ended up in a hospital bed. I felt a tremendous responsibility to "do it all" without interruption; I was trying to ensure that I met everyone's needs and, in the process, was neglecting my own.

You also were too young to remember when I suffered a miscarriage, for which I felt responsible, and your father and I didn't know if we would ever be able to have another child. You don't know how the same day I was told that news, I attended a news conference for one of our players headed to the WNBA and pushed myself to look happy during one of the saddest moments in my life. Pictures in the newspaper the next day showed my bloodshot eyes—I had gone directly from the doctor's office to the press conference.

You might recall how your dad and I have talked about my serious car wreck that took place shortly before we were married. I was driving to work when I was an assistant coach at Auburn, and got distracted and ran off the road. I still don't know how I avoided any serious injury, or worse. As you turn 17 and become old enough to drive—independently and all over the country—my own personal experiences cause me to worry so much about you. I also worry about your health, because a couple of years ago, I was diagnosed with melanoma—another humbling challenge in which life sometimes can move on without you, and only a sense of life and faith can direct you.

Those experiences are what I want to share in this book. I want you to understand my life, and in the process, *your* life. Your grandmother is British and did not have the opportunity to finish college; however, she remains one of the smartest women I know. She made the difficult choice to move her family from Florida back to Maine, and even though it was a long distance away from your grandfather's job as a Navy pilot, she did it—all because she thought it was a much better place to raise her family. As one of her three children, I had no idea how hard that must have been for her; and now, as a mother, I cannot imagine what it was like having to make that decision.

You were still a young girl when we had the opportunity to move from Maine and I became the basketball coach at Michigan State. You grew up in Michigan, made a lot of friends, and really enjoyed life there. That was why you were so devastated when, at the age of 13, your happy world was torn apart when the offer came for me to coach the women's team at Duke. Your father and I believed moving to new places was beneficial to your growth. As a daughter of a Navy pilot (your "Papa") when I was young, his career ensured that moving was simply a part of the fabric of what we did. The difference is that my mom and dad never moved their children again after age 14, 15, or so. We knew this would be your last move until high school graduation. We hoped you would learn a great deal along the way.

While I don't have to remind you how unhappy you were the first year we lived in Durham, you don't know how much I carried your sadness with me, and how badly I hurt for you. I tried to sort through what I had done to you. It was truly a bittersweet moment when your former high school team in East Lansing won the state championship that season—a joy you would have experienced had we remained there. My thoughts kept drifting back to the decision your grandmother made: moving her family back to Maine because she knew it was the right thing to do. I worried that I had done exactly the opposite. Was I hurting my family because of my own desire to pursue the ultimate job? Had my yearning to go against the grain and take a new job when our family was so entrenched in Michigan been the wrong decision? Was I compromising my family instead of trying to improve all of our lives?

There were many nights that year, when I was off recruiting and found myself alone in a silent hotel room, that I cried for you. I could not escape the fact that I had disrupted your world, nor could I evade the guilt I felt. We saw the move as a tremendous opportunity for you to reinvent yourself—to create your world without it being created for you. So much of your Michigan life was comfortable and connected to your mom, "the coach."

Your world was tied to mine because of my profession. People recognized you because of what I did. I didn't realize how painful it would be for me to see you suffering so much. It was a hurtful process to observe as a parent. We had to stay patient, but we had to let you create your own new world in Durham.

Of course, it really hit both of us hard that next year when the NCAA decided how much fun it would be to send the Duke team to the regional tournament hosted by Michigan State and a probable second-round matchup between the former coach and her former team. I know exactly what the NCAA was doing, and I didn't like it. It became about "the coach returning" rather than the two talented teams, and it added unnecessary drama. It wasn't fair to either my old players or to the Duke players. You were excited watching the pairings show when the news flashed on the television. You got an unexpected trip back to East Lansing and a chance to hang out again with your friends.

Then the game came—one that we played in a terribly hostile environment. Michigan State played incredibly well, and they beat us. We got on the plane to fly back to Durham, and you and I huddled and cried. You cried so hard, and I tried to hold you and tell you it would be okay. The players were farther back in the plane and didn't see us; and even though a lot of the administrators and coaches saw us crying, I didn't mind. I was a mother at that moment, not a coach.

Finally, you dried some of your tears and looked up at me and said, "How could they do that to you? How could those people not love my mother and be grateful for what you did there?" We started crying again—poignant thoughts and a remarkable time for us to grow.

You didn't realize it then, but that was the day you said good-bye to Michigan. That moment allowed you to be free and move on with your life.

I hope and pray that you are happy now. You were able to find a new school that you enjoy, make new friends, and reinvent yourself in a beautiful new state. You really have no idea how proud of you your father and I are.

Becoming a coach was not a decision I made easily. When your father and I got married, we knew we wanted two children, and we knew the demands that would be placed on both of us. Most female coaches who have children traditionally stay at the same school for their entire career. It was unusual for me to leave Maine and go to Michigan State, and it was almost unprecedented to leave a program like that for the job at Duke—a Top 10 team and a traditional power. Yet I did it because it was the job I always wanted, the job I thought I had been pursuing without even knowing it.

Your mom is a Title IX baby and a pioneer in women's basketball—someone who is operating in uncharted territory. Our family's visions and dreams seemed to be a bit more complicated than most. Replacing a legendary coach just does not easily happen in women's basketball. Coaches generally go to one school and stay there for the rest of their careers as they work toward building that particular program. A coach who leaves one Top 20 program to coach another Top 10 team is a rare circumstance; it doesn't take place often enough for many to accept and understand such a change. It is truly a new and exciting world to conquer.

I want you to know that while it is rewarding, leadership can be lonely. I am not the first coach or business executive who has come to understand that. I've come to accept that a sense of isolation comes with the job; but that doesn't make it any easier. These demands can make a person more or less secluded, depending on who they are. There is a natural propensity in leadership to withdraw at times. When this happens, the question then becomes: How quickly can you reengage in your work with your people to move the whole forward under various circumstances?

I know there were times when I withdrew that affected our entire family. My leadership skills were challenged in trying to find the balance between my passion for my work and my passion for family. Without question, I think I have learned how to do this more effectively, and I hope you can find that proper balance, too. Achieving this makes life feel extremely fulfilling, puts everybody in a great place, and allows your family to benefit so much from your career.

Take this morning, for example. Your father and brother are playing in a tennis tournament, and it was up to me to make sure they had all of the paperwork completed and took it with them when they left. After trying to get in a short run, I took you to your SAT preparation class. Then I had to meet two recruits who were visiting Duke for breakfast, and I was receiving text message updates of Jack's tennis match while we were eating. Multitasking was once again my word of the day. The work never stops—as a wife, parent, or coach—and your support and under-standing are always greatly appreciated.

I learned a valuable lesson when I was in college at Northwestern: that whiners never get anywhere in life. I honestly believe that people who want to be happy and positive should consciously separate them-selves from people who are always negative. You need to seek out others who have similar values to your own, who make a difference in life, and who make a difference in the lives of others despite the challenges at hand. These are the people who earn and have a high quality of life—the things for which our family has always searched. That's the kind of person I want you to be as an adult—someone who is positive and happy, somebody who loves her life, who lives it without regrets and with purpose, who thinks and feels deeply along the way.

I would not change anything in my life even if I could—except maybe for the results of a couple of games over the years.

I hope that reading this book will give a better understanding of me, my world, and your life as you know it today. I want you—and everybody else who reads it—to identify with the process that's involved in what I do. The phrase "balancing your life" has always seemed to be a cliché to me; or perhaps it's just part of the challenge. I focus my life much more intensely on finding a way to restore energy. And the way I do that is with passion—for everything I do. I want to love the process and celebrate the choices I have made throughout my life.

I want my experiences to be a lesson for you and everyone else who reads this book who are trying to be successful in their jobs, marriages, or as parents, coaches, mentors, or children.

If you, or anybody else, can learn something from what has hap-pened in my life, it will make me very happy. Your father and I want the best for you, because you deserve it. We want you to pursue your dreams, celebrate your sense of life, and allow your own choices to bring you wonderful health and happiness. And, as always, love your brother.

X's and O's
Love,
Mom

Coach P's daughter, Maddie, in Maine during the summer of 2010.
Source: Personal Collection

1

BE READY FOR CHANGE AND ADVENTURE

OPPORTUNITY KNOCKS

My husband John and I were standing in the kitchen of our home in East Lansing, Michigan, in March of 2007 when our lives changed forever.

John and I had been discussing the fact that it did not seem like I would ever be able to leave to coach another women's basketball team. Because my Michigan State contract was quite restrictive, it did not appear that there was any chance we could ever leave the state or that I'd have the freedom to work anywhere else.

Being in a place where you *want* to be forever is one thing; however, being told you can *never leave* that place is another matter entirely. John and I were confused and physically tired after the unsuccessful contract negotiations. We felt that we had made a tremendous effort to try to find a solution and had finally come to the conclusion that we were going to respect what we could not control and make the best of it. We were rationalizing by focusing on the fact that we loved our neighbors, we loved the town of East Lansing, and we had an incredible team with players I loved who were returning to school. John truly thought I was meant to coach that team; so we had come to the conclusion that perhaps a move just wasn't in the cards or something we could control at that time.

I was upbeat and excited to move forward. We really had come full circle. Interestingly, there was a calm peace about our conversation that day. We had stood up for our principles, relative to our large buyout, and we felt good about our attempt to make things better and right. Since we had completed seven great years there, we felt we had earned such freedom and overall support.

We literally were in the middle of contemplating our situation when the discussion was interrupted by a telephone call from Jacki Silar, the longtime administrator of women's sports at Duke. Jacki had been an assistant coach on the women's basketball team when Duke was recruiting me as a player in high school. Since I had spoken to her all those years ago, it felt like a long-lost friend calling. And yet again, she was calling with an invitation: to ask me if I had any interest in becoming the women's basketball coach at Duke, a job which had recently become vacant. If I had been sitting down, I would have fallen out of my chair.

The timing of the call was as overwhelming as the prospect of coaching at Duke. I was as excited as I had ever been; it almost felt divine. John and I actually started laughing, since we could not believe the timing. Of course, John had no idea who I was talking to when I answered the phone, despite the fact that I was pointing to the phone and mouthing the words "Duke, Duke." He was shaking his head back and forth with a big smile on his face.

It was not a long conversation; Jacki just wanted to know if I would be interested in the job. Though I thought about my Michigan State players, I convinced myself that they would be better off without me and might benefit from having a different coach. I wondered if I could be as productive with administrators at the school, and whether everybody's relationships could heal. I knew that my spirit was damaged, and that those feelings could potentially be passed on to my players. Coaches are only as good as their own health and the support around them. If you don't feel comfortable in the situation you're in, then it's tough—almost impossible—to be an effective coach. I had pushed the envelope so far I didn't know if it could heal properly; I knew that if that didn't happen, the players would get hurt in the long run. The kids were never the reason I wanted to leave. In fact, I knew that we were leaving a gold mine, and potentially my second Final Four team.

As far as I was concerned, it had to do with taking responsibility as a leader. I knew that I had gotten into a not-so-positive contractual situation. I also knew that healing definitely needed to take place, and I worried whether this was compromising my players in any way. It was a classic case of a parent wanting to protect her kids. With this weighing on my mind, another opportunity surfaced—so I thought maybe this was what was meant to be. I needed to leave so the players could enjoy a new coach with no contractual or relationship issues.

A leader must evaluate a global view as well as the individual fit within the working environment. I refer to this as *collateral damage*; you can win your argument but lose out in the long run. What we learned from the situation was to control what we could; perhaps even more important, I learned to read and understand the long-term consequences of contracts. The buyout clause was haunting to me in terms of my future, my freedom, and a sense of trust.

Coaching is a very humbling profession, since we truly are all replaceable as coaches. The challenge I was facing only reinforced this point of view. If a school and a coach have principles that don't line up, then difficulties can arise, which was the case in this situation. Like coaches, many business leaders are a product of their relationships. Though it's critical to be a person of principle with a strong belief in your philosophy, your relationships with people are also hugely significant. You have to be careful and understand what—and where—you are willing to compromise in order to move forward most efficiently.

The trials and tribulations of being a coach at a major university are not limited to men's sports. Like any executive in the business world today, women are just as involved as men in life-changing decisions. I know, because it has happened to me.

I was born and reared to be ready for change and adventure. I was always comfortable being the new kid in class. As one of my former high school teachers would later write on my college applications, "Joanne has that rare quality of not fearing being wrong or incorrect when she speaks in class." I always felt that was a thoughtful and very humorous comment to share with all my future college contacts and student-athletes. But it's the truth; I have never been afraid to be wrong. This easy acceptance has helped me grow faster than most people. In fact, I attribute becoming a head coach at the tender age of 26 to this willingness to share information. I consider my naïveté to be an advantage, because it enabled me to drop my guard and listen and learn—whether I was right or wrong. Some folks make the mistake in business of taking a title and letting it control them, especially when they are young. I was excited about my title, but I was definitely a people-driven person. I knew the importance of seeking out older, more experienced folks for advice and to bounce ideas off of regularly.

As a product of a British mom and a mostly Italian naval pilot father, I was always ready to travel almost anywhere. I learned a great deal about survival and fighting through tough times; I've had more than my fair share of handling conflicts and change through transitions and life lessons.

I found out later in life all of those lessons would be quite valuable to me as a college basketball coach.

Even though Duke had called me, I was not immediately offered the coaching job. I had to go visit the campus in Durham, North Carolina, and meet with the committee that would be selecting the coach. I was excited, unsure, motivated—and taking an enormous risk, since Duke had not actually offered me the job. Additionally, the MSU community was not looking favorably on me for engaging in the Duke search.

My First Meeting with Coach K

Duke officials had sent me my itinerary not long before I was to depart for Durham; much to my disappointment, I saw that a meeting with men's basketball coach Mike Krzyzewski was not on it. I learned early in my career that it is extremely beneficial to have a good rapport and productive relationship with all the athletic programs, but especially with the men's basketball programs. There is no reason why both men's and women's programs cannot be mutually beneficial to one another.

It could be said that I had a very productive working relationship with the men's basketball coach at both the University of Maine and Michigan State. Tom Izzo, at MSU, had taught me to pay attention to great detail and to value a championship coach. With Coach K, I was valuing the very best coach in the business.

Additionally, Coach K is the most influential person in terms of Duke's basketball program and perhaps the greatest coach in the history of the sport. I was not going to get on the plane to fly to Durham without being absolutely sure I was to meet with the person responsible for building Duke into a worldwide basketball power.

To this day, I don't know whether it was Joe Alleva, the athletic director who hired me, or Jacki Silar who set up the meeting with Mike. As it turned out, Coach K was leaving Durham early to begin his USA Basketball duties on the same day I was there. Mike graciously agreed to meet early, at 8:00 AM, just before he took off for his trip.

In retrospect, I was happy with the choice I made about my decision to include Coach K on my itinerary. The impromptu itinerary change may have caused the Duke officials to have been taken aback somewhat since the request was unusual, but I felt good that I had the fortitude and the wherewithal to do what I thought was the right thing to do. At the time of making that decision, I had to check my emotions, stay reasonable, and come up with a solution; and I didn't have a lot of time. Much like calling a certain play in a time and score situation at the end of the game, I hoped I had not only made the right call but had enough time on the clock to execute.

I looked forward to our meeting; I had read Coach K's books throughout my entire coaching career (in fact, I felt I could quote them) and was extremely comfortable meeting him. I was not concerned with whether we'd have something to talk about. I knew that when you can think logically, embrace reason, stay cool—what some people in this day and age call "keeping it real"—then good things can happen. I was immensely excited to get on the plane.

At 8 AM, I walked into Coach K's office and sat down. We talked for more than an hour, and he raised a question at one point: "I understand you have not officially been offered the job?" My reply was, "No, I have not." With a little higher intonation in his voice—and in a slow, firm statement of care—he asked, "What are you doing here, then?"

It was simply the way he asked that made me think about the question myself. He was interjecting the thought about caring for my entire career and seeing the whole rather than just this part—my attempt to become the coach at Duke. He understood what was happening to me without my telling or even alluding to the facts of what had happened at Michigan State. He was putting the care piece for me ahead of Duke.

Coach K knew my situation at Michigan State, as well as the risk I was taking by coming to Durham without an official job offer. He asked if he could walk with me to my next meeting, and of course I agreed to his extraordinary gesture. We left his office on the sixth floor and went down to the media room on the first floor, where the hiring committee was meeting. He asked me to remain in the hall as he went into the room to talk to the group.

Though I never found out what Coach K said to the committee, I did learn later that he had explained how a coach with my credentials should not have been placed in this position, and he explained the risk I was taking by even being on the Duke campus. He tried to help the committee members understand my situation—and what I was willing to do to get this job.

Mike came out of the room a short while later. He wished me well with my candidacy and gave his regards to my family, then gave me a quick hug. Excited about leaving to coach the USA basketball team, he wished me well and said he hoped to see me at Duke.

Mike's leadership on that morning was an act of random kindness and support. He will never know or understand how much that meant to me—and how it impressed me beyond measure as a coach attempting such a bold personal and professional move.

Whether it was Mike's talk to the committee that convinced them to offer me the job, I will never know. But they did. I said yes, and after days filled with clouds and fog, my world was sunny, bright, and very busy once again.

Ever since I was a young girl growing up in Maine, I had an intense desire to be the best I could be. I wanted to take advantage of every opportunity I was given. I wanted my life to be what *I* wanted it to be, not what somebody else wanted it to be. Without even realizing it at the time, my desire was to live my life by choice, not chance. I have tried to do that ever since, and so far, it's worked out pretty well.

The choice to coach at Duke was an awe-inspiring leap of faith to truly test my abilities at the highest level of the women's game. A motivated, excited, proud, and humbled pioneering spirit churned inside of me as I realized how much there was to do and learn.

Coach P being interviewed outside the locker room of Cameron Indoor Stadium during the 2010 NCAA Tournament First-Round Media Day on March 19, 2010. Duke hosted the first and second rounds of the 2010 NCAA Tournament.
Source: Duke Photography

CHAPTER 1 QUESTIONS

- The first chapter deals with a major change in my family's and my life. How have you handled change lately?
- What recent examples of leadership in your life have been lonely or challenging?
- When you have entered new adventures or challenges in your life, what have you done to understand the value of the people who came before you?
- During times of transition or in the face of adversity, what have you done to stick to your principles?
- When in your professional and personal life have you stated what you need and negotiated for it appropriately?

2

CREATING "CHOICE NOT CHANCE"

WE ARE ALL PRODUCTS OF THE CHOICES WE MAKE

When I was coaching at Maine, we created a program called "Choice Not Chance," which stemmed from a philosophy that I thoroughly believe in and endorse. My mantra is simple: "Choice, not chance, determines destiny. Choose to become a champion in life."

We had a big white blank wall outside our offices on the third floor, and I knew I wanted to put something on that wall where everybody could see it. I was only 26, and as the youngest head coach in Division I basketball at that time, philosophy was very important to me. You had to stare at that wall when you left my office. Some people would have covered it with photos or pictures, but I wanted to use a quote, and the preceding quote was the one I used. I am certain I must have read it someplace, but I honestly have no idea where it came from. It just seemed to appear, and the blank wall was a perfect spot for it.

I came up with five components of the philosophy that grew out of the quote. I didn't realize how much it would evolve over time. It pushed me to think further and broaden the philosophy to the point where those elements are now a fixture of Choice Not Chance. Developing each of these five components has truly been an evolutionary process:

1. Choices dictate life's opportunities, so make choices with great care.

2. Your "little choices" *do* matter. You must commit daily to seeking out the right choices for yourself, and operate according to a belief system that all of your choices *do matter.*

3. It is crucial to practice "right thinking," which means to "think deeply, think clearly, and allow yourself to feel deeply." All of these are part of the process of making reasonable choices.

4. Keep your power. Recognize that you are in control, and continue to develop your "power" further. Incorporate a mind-set to "stay in the moment" to fortify self-determination and your power to perform.

5. "If it's meant to be, it's up to me." Always remain focused, and embrace reason over emotion at all costs.

From that quote, "If it's meant to be, it's up to me," we developed CNC (Choice Not Chance) Ballclub for both boys and girls of all ages from eighth grade and below, to support the program. After I started coaching, this philosophy became incredibly important; I had seen too many folks play victim to life's ups and downs and act as if life weren't a matter of choice. I always wanted young folks to know that *they* were in charge—and that the choices they made did have power.

It's important for a coach to study the X's and O's; however, CNC became my major philosophy and way of thinking. It's not a fist like Coach K uses, and it's not John Wooden's pyramid, but it's a way of thinking that I established with my teams as the right way to approach almost anything—in basketball and in life. I remind them constantly that we are in charge, we are in control, and we have power to change our lives. Kids are born into a variety of circumstances; I emphasize to them as strongly as I can that they are not victims of the circumstances into which they were born. Rather, I teach that you are a victim of the choices you make. That simple distinction literally changes their attitude and energy. Young people begin to realize they can make choices that are as simple as doing homework or loving and honoring their parents. The thrust of my entire coaching philosophy is about understanding those choices, as well as the fact that each person is in charge of his or her own destiny. All of this was something that was critical for me to teach to my team and carry over into the community. And it has taken off everyplace we've been.

The principal idea of CNC is to share a method of thinking that can help young folks sort through life's challenges and distractions, giving them a sense of control and purpose.

I wanted everyone in the communities in which I coached to think about how we are all a product of the choices we make. Even the youngest kids make choices every day: Do they brush their teeth in the morning? Do they make their bed? Do they choose to do their homework or their chores? These are the decisions that put you, and keep you, in charge of your destiny. You have power; you must keep it and develop it.

I talk to my teams all the time about keeping their power. To me, those terms almost imply that you are creating a brand for yourself— a powerful brand indeed.

We incorporated the philosophy into the summer camps we did with young girls. I wanted them to learn early on that the choices they made were what would prevent their lives from being subject to chance. It starts with very simple, basic, everyday decisions like getting exercise and eating right. I wanted them to think it was cool to eat bananas, apples, and oranges, get their homework done before watching television, or work on their basketball skills in the driveway before going inside.

I love to develop people so that their actions allow them to feel better about themselves. My goal for the campers, for my own two kids, and for all of my teams is for them to be the very best they can be. And that starts with the things we control—the choices that we get to make in life. Without making solid choices, the work you do is diminished, and your personal productivity quotient decreases; in other words, you lose the connection between your actions driving your productivity.

I carried that philosophy with me from Maine to Michigan State and on to Duke, but I honestly believe it should apply to everyone everywhere, not just to the players who happen to be on my basketball team.

When you are young, parents and teachers are usually the ones who tell you what to do. As you grow, those role models fade into the background and you are left to make decisions on your own. But if you have received proper training about how to make good choices, you are taking the chance part out of your future and increasing the odds that you'll lead a successful and productive life.

Being a college basketball coach gives me the opportunity to work with young adults, as well as younger children over the summer. What I often see from both groups is a lack of motivation or desire to improve. Even if they do want to improve, they let the wrong kind of thinking hinder their ability to do so. This doesn't just happen on the basketball court; it takes places in life in general. One of a coach's most important jobs is to motivate, encourage, and bring out the best in his or her players. Passion and a sense of life are critical to growth for anyone. And there's an important lesson to keep in mind here:

The best motivators don't have to be coaches.

They merely have to be honest, authentic, and real people—individuals who have an incredible passion for their job and for life.

I am reminded daily that "Choice Not Chance" is a winning philosophy by looking at my own life, and the decisions that I have made over the years, beginning when I was a young girl.

The decisions we make as we grow up are always challenging, and sometimes even volatile. Despite individual circumstances that vary so greatly among us all, whatever your conditions or your situation, you can seek control and power—as long as you are open to growth and personal improvement and you evaluate choices along the way.

Coach P with her first freshman class at Duke, the Class of 2011 (Jasmine Thomas, Karima Christmas, and Krystal Thomas), during summer camp in 2010. Players are coaches at Coach P's summer camp to help instill the principles of "Choice Not Chance" in campers.
Source: Personal Collection

CHAPTER 2 QUESTIONS

- What are some of the best choices you've made in your life?
- Do you have choices you regret or learned from in your life? What are they?
- Do you often leave things to chance?
- What choices in your life motivate you?

CHOICE NOT CHANCE

3

THE UNDERDOG, FIGHTER MENTALITY

A Navy Brat Grows Up

My life likely would have been much different if I had not been a kid from Maine. I honestly believe that—for a lot of reasons.

I am the middle child of Christina and Robert Palombo; my father was a pilot, so I am also a Navy brat. Like almost all children who are born into a military family, we moved several times when I was young. Although I was born in California, we moved to Brunswick, Maine, before I was old enough to start school and lived there until I had completed the fourth grade.

A new assignment in Jacksonville, Florida, interrupted our life at that time—and for a year, my parents, older brother, younger sister, and I left our happy home in Maine. I was in the fifth grade, and that honestly was one of the most difficult years of my life.

I couldn't seem to find anything I was good at, and sports was not a focal point in my life. I played soccer and ran track, but was mostly just an average kid; in fact, *average* was the word I kept using to identify myself. I felt that I didn't do anything with any degree of excellence, nor did I feel connected to or engaged in anything substantial. My life just seemed so *basic*. I can still remember standing by a pool in 1976, an Olympic year. I watched athletes like Nadia Comaneci and Mark Spitz, and was amazed by their success. My mom signed me up for a swim team to keep me busy, and since we had a pool, I would swim back and forth across that pool even though I was only an average swimmer. I was watching the Olympics at the same time, and I really thought I could be part of the games one day—even though there was absolutely no evidence of that ever being a possibility. The Olympic spirit was very clearly a part of me at that time. And although I could not find a sport to realistically lead me there, I knew it was something I wanted to do.

Years later, when I was coaching USA Basketball and won gold medals in Mexico City and Moscow, we were training in Colorado Springs. I walked into my hotel room and saw all of this USA gear laid out on my bed. I was all by myself, but it was one of the greatest moments in my coaching career. I became emotional about representing our country, and called my parents on the telephone to share the moment with them. It's funny how quickly those pool memories of 1976 could flood back so quickly. The pride I had to be a USA coach was overwhelming.

Being in the fifth grade was a strange time for me; I think the word that best describes how I felt is *hollow*. I was pretty much a lost puppy.

My brother, who is two years older than me, was also struggling to adapt to our move to Florida, an area where kids grew up too fast. One day he was actually frisked on his way into school, and one of my classmates tried to get me to smoke in the bathroom at school. I don't know whether it was those incidents that prompted my parents to realize Florida was not the place where they wanted to raise their children, but they made a pivotal decision that we were moving back to Brunswick, Maine, after a year.

This was not an easy decision, because my father still had to work in Jacksonville. He had to commute home, and because of the expense of trying to maintain two homes, our life in Maine, from a strictly financial point of view, was not ideal. We left a nice home in a Jacksonville suburb with a swimming pool and moved back to a small home in Brunswick where the kids slept on cots. We had fewer material things, but everybody was so much happier that it was worth making those sacrifices. That was a crucial lesson for me in realizing how limiting material items can be. I could just *feel* the unhappiness during the year we spent in Jacksonville—and that feeling disappeared when we moved back to Maine.

What I realized years later, of course, was how my parents made the biggest sacrifice involved in that move. They decided that going back to Maine was the best thing they could do for their children's happiness and future. If my British mum had not been such a strong woman, I don't think she ever could have attempted to raise and care for three young children while my father was working so far away.

Having traveled around the world because of basketball, and having been involved with a lot of parents and children, I realize how blessed I am to have the parents I have. Our parents always put their children first. My mother realized that Brunswick, Maine, was the best place she knew of to raise her children. It was small-town America at its finest, with the work ethic and values consistent with my parents' beliefs.

WHEREVER THEY LIVE, KIDS NEED TO BE MOTIVATED

My parents did something incredibly important while I was growing up: They realized the importance of small-town principles. I am not saying everyone has to move to rural Indiana or Maine to have happy and successful children; however, I do think it's essential, even in the largest cities in the country, for parents to find a way to create that supportive, small-town environment for their families. Parents have to be involved in their children's lives; they have to find programs and activities that their kids enjoy; and they need to motivate them to work hard at whatever it is they like to do. Parents do not have to be overly involved to drive their children's athletic development; they simply have to provide opportunity and encouragement, and then let children develop their interests and talents naturally. The passion should come from the child, who is forever changed by the experience.

My parents did not push me or my brother or sister into sports; however, they supported our decisions and gave us every opportunity to decide for ourselves if whatever we were doing was something we wanted to pursue. I had absolutely no idea when I signed up to play intramural basketball in the sixth grade that I was becoming involved with a sport that would be with me decades later—and provide me with a lifetime of opportunity.

I had no skill set and had not played much basketball before, but somebody told me at the end of one game, "You just scored 28 points." I can literally remember my self-worth changing after receiving that comment, because I had found something I wanted to do, and it was something I did *well*. That was an earth-shattering, eye-opening, motivating, and exciting experience for me.

As I lay on the couch in the summer, watching television, I found myself thinking, *This just can't be it; there's got to be more.* The drumbeat in my head was very real, and I realized at that moment that the "more" for me was basketball. It got me outside and motivated. My dad put up a basketball hoop in our driveway, and I found myself outside for hours a day, just shooting baskets. Friends came by and asked what I was doing out there by myself; it almost seemed as though they thought it was strange, but it seemed perfectly normal to me, because I was doing exactly what I wanted to do. I was shooting, playing, getting wet with the hose, and playing until I was dry. That became my world.

I spent five hours every day over an entire summer with my own hoop. I find this important—and almost incredible—because so few people do this anymore. I have always believed that real discipline is doing what you don't want to do when you don't want to do it and doing it well. Without discipline, a person's craft can be truly compromised to the point of never finding out exactly what they can do. Very few aspiring ballplayers spend enough time in the gym or driveway alone, honing skills, making up games and pushing themselves to become better.

ROLE MODELS HELP ME DEVELOP MY SKILLS

Girls' basketball was a very popular sport at the high school level in Maine, and we had an organized team in middle school, complete with cheerleaders and fans. I was one of three seventh graders selected to play on the junior high team, and that was where my education in basketball really began. My junior high coach, Allen Graffam, must have seen something in me, and he took the time to work with me and encourage and motivate me. He taught me how to shoot. Once I learned how to do so properly, I flourished.

The importance of having a coach such as Coach Graffam was no doubt lost on me as a 13-year-old, but I recognize it now. He gave me a goal—to make the varsity team when I was a freshman—and told me that I could do it if I worked hard and dedicated myself. He opened the gym for us in the summer, gave me the opportunity to develop my skills, and showed me how good I could be.

My high school coach, Fred Koerber, was another excellent role model. He knew how badly I wanted to make the varsity team the summer before I entered high school. However, Coach Koerber was honest with me. He told me he was not going to just give me a spot on the team; I had to earn it, and I had to do so by outplaying all of the other kids on the team. I had to be one of the six best players or he would not give me a varsity spot.

I went to every little camp and practice program offered in the area. Our team spent much of the summer traveling in the coach's camper to scrimmage other teams around the state. We all piled in, drove two hours, scrimmaged, stopped at a lake to go swimming, went to McDonald's for dinner, and drove home. It was a classic summer and a great time for all.

This kind of simple life truly does help young people focus, trust, learn, and grow. That summer gave me the time I needed to improve as an aspiring player. It seems nowadays that there are too many tournaments, too many coaches who have so little time with the team, too much travel, and too many games. All of this produces tired, worn-out, noncompetitive kids who wonder whether they have gotten any better at all.

I think that the sense of connectedness I felt during those first years is (sadly) missing from summer ball now. Stars may shine at times, but many kids become lost or disillusioned about what practice and hard work really are on a daily basis. The world of youth sports has changed substantially over the years; I don't know whether kids get to have summers like I had anymore, and that's a shame. It was a healthy and wonderful way to grow up. My parents supported me, drove me to the camps, and gave me the chance I needed to be successful. The more frequently players attend national tournaments that draw teams from all over the country (and they come in many forms), the more games these kids play away from their high school teams. They attend more camps as individuals and fewer as teams. Though this creates more choices, it can sometimes force the experience of being on a cohesive team in high school into the backseat of a player's development.

I, however, had Coach Koerber, who made me play every other varsity player one-on-one. I had to beat every one of them in order to win the chance to play on the varsity team—and I did it. When I learned that I had made the team as a freshman, it was one of the happiest days of my life.

The Title IX legislation had been passed a few years earlier, calling for girls in high school and college to be given the same opportunities to play sports as boys. This legislation, although extremely pivotal to promoting girls and women in sports, was not something I was aware of at the time. At least at our school, Brunswick High, the girls' team was more popular and more successful than the boys' team. We drew so many fans to our games that they had to pull out both sides of the bleachers, while they had to pull out only one side for the boys' games.

In this way, I was fortunate enough to be a Title IX child ahead of my time. The environment where I grew up in Maine, which blessed me with all of my mentors, pushed me into believing that women should essentially expect to receive equal treatment and opportunity. I was oblivious to the idea that all people my age—and nationwide—did not share this belief.

We were a big show in town, and people came to watch us. Our best player was a senior named Rita O'Connor, and she was an incredible basketball player. My goal was to be like Rita. She was the most successful player in our school's history and was being recruited by a lot of Division I programs. The entire impetus behind my desire to play on varsity as a freshman was to play on the same team with Rita. I knew that it was the only year I would have that chance.

I remember telling my dad when he was driving me to one of those various camps around the state that, to thank him, I was going to earn a scholarship and he would not have to pay for me to go to college. He laughed and smiled in support, but I was serious.

Although I loved and found success while playing basketball, one thing I didn't do was forget about other sports. I might not have been as good at soccer or softball, or as talented in track, but I was involved in all of them. I think that's another mistake that kids and their parents make today—trying to decide too early to specialize in a particular sport at the expense of everything else. Multiple-sport athletes benefit from cross-training, greater balance in friendships, varied arenas in which to lead, and less overall burnout when training. If I had told my mom and dad that I was going to play only basketball while I was in high school, my dad would have immediately started asking me questions like, "Why? What's going on? You're a pretty good softball player."

He saw the value in being able to play multiple sports, something that is too often lost today.

I immediately take a liking to kids who tell me that they play multiple sports. I recruit those kids harder and I encourage them. It always seems to me that those individuals are the ones who have the greatest opportunity to be successful at the next level—college. The broader mind-set developed by kids who have cross-trained is usually an indication that they will not suffer from burnout.

The other mistake I see a lot of parents making in youth sports today is an attempt to be both a parent and a coach at the same time. One of the greatest reasons for my success was that my mom and dad didn't base their identity as parents on what I did as a child-athlete. Though they were incredibly supportive, it was *my* choice to play, not theirs. I was not playing to please them; I was doing it because it made me happy. Again, it was a choice, not a chance, created by my parents' desire. Kids who aren't given this choice are at risk for having their lives begin to spin out of control—simply because other people are trying to direct them and their choices. An individual of any age has to develop a motivation and a desire on his or her own. Nobody else can make that happen.

My father was busy flying Navy planes, and though my mother came to every game, she didn't say much else to me. My dad would rebound for me forever but he would never critique or coach me. It's different now; so many parents think they are (or should be) their kids' coach.

The kids who become successful college players today manage to do so because of the choices *they* make, not the choices that others make for them. Kids who get to college who have had other people making their choices for them their entire lives are the ones who go flat. They have difficulty meeting or exceeding expectations and can often have a loss of a sense of self, passion, and motivation. It makes much more sense to me to operate according to the maxim that you should "allow your children to choose, and then support their choices."

It is incredibly important to expose children to the option of sports. Parents must understand how to motivate their kids. For instance, I don't coach my daughter, Maddie, at all in basketball. I rebound for her; I help her ice her sore knee; and I support her in every way I'm able to and attend every game I can. I have very few discussions with Maddie about technique and basketball. I let her coaches coach her. I keep my Mom status with her.

One night, John and I went to dinner with Jack at the golf course. We were sitting outside near the putting green and it was a beautiful chance to spend some time putting and chipping. However, I knew that suggesting this to Jack would only prompt his contrarian personality to surface. So instead, I suggested to John that we take the putter and chipper with us to dinner. We didn't mention practicing; rather, we talked about what we were going to eat. Then barely two minutes after we sat down, Jack got up and said he was going to go putt and chip.

There is a true psychology for parents about how to teach their children and help nurture them—*without* getting in their way. After he got it into his head that he was going to practice, we could barely get Jack to come eat his dinner. He made up a game on the green to see how few putts it would take for him to connect all the holes. It was fascinating to watch. Jack didn't ask us to join him; he simply continued to play his game. We ate, smiled—and never went down there to interrupt him. We simply let him be.

NURTURING INTEREST AND A DESIRE TO IMPROVE

My parents were in the stands supporting me all through high school. Their encouragement was a major reason why I was able to find success in basketball, because it kept me working harder to improve. When anybody, especially a child, has an interest in something, it has to be nurtured or that interest will fade away.

Another advantage I had—one that I see missing in so many youth sports today—was quality coaching. Sometimes when I'm out recruiting or watching one of my children play, I see coaches making complete fools of themselves by screaming and acting totally of out control. These individuals have no idea what they are doing or how to coach. I want to stand up and scream myself—not at the coaches, but at the parents who let coaches get away with all of the negative ranting.

It all comes down to accountability. Parents can't look the other way. A is A; that's logical, reasonable thinking. You know it when you see it, and parents need to take back the power. If they don't, the situation can quickly become unhealthy.

I will always be grateful for Coach Koerber's faith in me: When I was a freshman, he even had the guts to put me in the starting lineup ahead of a senior, because he believed I had earned the position. He allowed me to play guard, despite the fact that I was tall enough to play inside, because he knew that would be my best position in the future. I was already a perfectionist who wanted everything in my life to be just so, and Coach Koerber was able to put up with that when a lot of coaches would have objected. Most of all, he made the game *fun* for everybody on our team. Life did not get any better than that summer when we traveled all over the state, scrimmaging, swimming in the lake, and eating at McDonald's. I hate to think about the kids today who are missing out on the opportunity to do things like this, who don't have the chance to realize that the true joy of sports comes from playing, and from the relationships that develop as a result.

I played one of my best high school games ever during my freshman year. I scored 18 points in the first half (and this was before the three-point shot was added). I can remember how very comfortable I felt, operating in a calm, confident state of mind. It was the first time I really ever experienced what sportscasters call "being in the zone." It was almost Zen-like—and I thought it was really cool.

Of course, the other team, which had been keying on Rita, started paying more attention to me in the second half. I think I finished the game with 24 points, and that was an instance in which I learned about true reality. It had been a great game, and my teammates had paved the way, too, but the second half presented a new challenge. It was one of the first times I learned about how life truly does have many different "halves," each with its own circumstances and trials.

I was lucky to grow up in an era when there were many talented female players in Maine who were attracting national attention from college coaches. One of the players who had come along a few years before me, Barb Krause, had played at Duke, and she was the person who first mentioned my name to the Duke coaches. Almost ironically, the first recruiting letter I received as a freshman in high school came from Duke.

The summer between my sophomore and junior years in high school changed my life. Since both boys' and girls' basketball was really popular in Maine, a businessman from Portland named Chris Smith decided that he wanted to sponsor two teams on a trip to play in an international tournament in Taiwan. I was selected for the team, and we were away from home for close to a month. It was the first time in my life I had been that far away from home without a parent, and the experience taught me a great deal about how to be independent. Some of the things I learned included how to travel with a girls' and boys' team; how to live in a hotel with a roommate; the importance of getting enough rest before games; how crucial it was to eat well, despite the food challenges I faced by being in another country and culture; the difficulty of being away from my parents; and how to manage the partying that could develop in the hotels. Once again, it was all about making the right choices in each situation.

We played against some great competition, which always makes you better, and the boys' Maine team actually won the tournament. The girls' team didn't win (but we should have).

It was the first time I had ever been in a foreign country, and I was only 15 years old. I had a roommate, and the issues around food that arose while I was away caused me to lose weight. There were social issues that had to do with being around the guys' team and having to make responsible decisions. This time away from home gave me an education about developing nutritious eating habits, the importance of getting enough sleep, the real need to be responsible with your time, and the value of establishing authentic social relationships.

We stopped in Hawaii on the way home, and I kept thinking that I had never done anything like that—and that basketball had made it possible. It was overwhelming, exciting, and thrilling to me. I was able to see how all of the work I had put in and the sacrifices I had made were now worth it because of this trip and the experiences I had enjoyed. I learned the important lesson that if you find your craft, dedicate yourself to it, and make it special, you won't believe the people you will meet and the places you will see.

The experience reminds me of some of the passages from my favorite book, Dr. Suess's *Oh, the Places You'll Go!* Though it's a children's book, the claims within it ring true no matter what your age; you will go to faraway places and do amazing things, all because you are committed to your sport, craft, or passion. Not only was this trip the experience of a lifetime, but it also allowed my basketball ability to go through the roof.

That trip set the stage for my final two years in high school, a time when my only real disappointment was not being able to win a state championship.

GRADUATION APPROACHES

I was hooked on basketball by this time; I had become a huge Larry Bird fan and watched him and the Boston Celtics play every chance I got. College basketball was not as popular then as it is now (thanks to all of the games being shown on ESPN). In fact, there really was very limited coverage of women's college basketball; but I was in front of my television watching the men's tournament every March. That's how a high school girl from Maine fell in love with Jim Valvano.

I cannot tell you why, but there was something about Valvano and his team, the North Carolina State Wildcats, that fascinated me. I was sitting in our living room watching on television when Lorenzo Charles rebounded Derek Wittenberg's missed shot and made the basket that gave NC State the championship in 1983, a couple of months before I graduated from high school. Actually, I was no longer sitting by that point in the game; I was jumping up and down and running around our living room, almost the same way Jimmy V was running all over the court, looking for somebody to hug.

Recruiting was far different in the early 1980s than it is today, given all of the technological advantages that the Internet provides. Yet college coaches from around the country somehow found out about me and began calling. I was named to the all-state team three times, and averaged 27 points a game as a junior. My average fell to 18 points as a senior, but our team went 20 and 2. A lot of coaches from some pretty prestigious schools showed up to watch me play. I really did not get caught up in that whole experience, probably because there was much less media attention and exposure than there is today. I remember one coach wanted to talk to me after we had lost a game, and I really was not interested. My parents, the coach, and I were sitting in our living room, and all I could think was, *Can I go now?* I was far more interested in playing the games.

When my mother realized that these coaches were serious about offering me a scholarship, she was very clear that she wanted me to get the best value I could. She wanted me to receive the best education possible, which was far more important to her than my playing basketball. She believed that private colleges and universities offered the best education, so she was determined I was going to go to a private school. She told me in her British accent, "Joanne, you must get the very best."

I admired my mother and did not question her thinking; I actually thought it was extremely helpful, since it would narrow down the schools I could attend and make the decision simpler. My mother is a brilliant woman; it amazed me how quickly she recognized that the scholarship needed to reflect something very valuable. She was thoughtful, and she taught me to be really grateful and to appreciate what these schools were offering me.

Perhaps my mother recognized the importance of these schools' quality because she did not have the opportunity to finish college. She always stressed to my sister and me that she wanted us to become strong, independent women who would never have to rely on anybody. Her selections had nothing to do with basketball; they were completely focused on the value of the scholarship. As such, she gave me the list and told me those were the only schools I could consider. She picked the very best schools (all private universities), and I didn't argue with her. My mother wanted me to have a better life than she had and to control my destiny, and I took her advice.

I wasn't sure what I wanted my major to be, which complicated the decision of trying to pick a school. My final four choices came down to Duke, Northwestern, Boston College, and Holy Cross. Though I was excited about picking a school, the whole recruiting experience was not that thrilling. One coach hung up the telephone on me when I told her I was going somewhere else. I had to leave soccer practice early to drive with my parents to Holy Cross for a visit, and I was more upset about leaving practice early than looking forward to the trip.

My parents were both busy when I made my visit to Duke, and I suspect that had a lot to do with my final decision about where I was going to go to school. It also was my first trip, so I didn't really know what to expect; even though I liked the school and had a great visit, I think the fact that my mother wasn't there really would have made it difficult for me if I'd told her I wanted to go to Duke.

My mom did go with me to Northwestern, and to their credit, the coaches there immediately picked up on how influential she was going to be in my decision. They did a great job of recruiting the heck out of my mother. When it came time to make the final choice, it was Northwestern. It sounds a little crazy, but it honestly didn't matter to me. I said okay; it was as simple as that. We did not have a news conference at the school and there was no dramatic announcement. I received the scholarship letter in the mail, signed it, and sent it back. That was all there was to it.

It was very hard for me to say no to Duke. The coaches there were disappointed, but very gracious about my decision.

Despite my recruitment and the exciting opportunities ahead, my mom always kept things in perspective. One night she even gave me a glimpse of what a "no scoreboard" mentality was all about. We were in the parking lot after a game at Mount Ararat High School in Maine, and she was, correctly, quietly scolding me for not taking a technical free throw seriously even though we were in a blowout game. I had missed the shot because of my silliness and lack of concentration, and Mom thought that was terribly inappropriate. During this disagreement, I emphatically stated, "I'm going to Duke and never coming back." Her point was that if I had been selected by my team to take the technical foul shots, I owed it to the team to concentrate and to try to make the shots, no matter what the game score was.

It was a lesson in no scoreboard mentality—that the score doesn't matter. You should always try your best.

One development during my senior year, which once again proved to me the power of motivation, occurred when I was named to the *Parade* magazine's High School All-America team. I was the first player ever selected from the state of Maine. It was a great honor, and I truly appreciated it; however, there were 40 players named to the team, and I was number 40. And my name was spelled wrong. That made me so mad, but it also motivated me.

I know that the misspelling was a simple and honest mistake, but I took it personally. As I headed off to college, I had already developed that underdog, fighter mentality that was going to stay with me forever.

Coach P holding the net following the 2010 ACC Championship Game against North Carolina State on March 7, 2010 in Greensboro, North Carolina.
Source: Duke Photography

CHAPTER 3 QUESTIONS

- All of us have had challenging years in our lives. During your challenging times, what did you learn?

- Have you ever observed sacrifices in someone else's life, or lived them? How did those sacrifices alter how you lead your life?

- Are you a healthy parent in terms of involvement with your kids? What do you do to consciously stay involved in your children's lives?

- Do you have a role model in your life? What do you look for in the role models in your life?

- Are you a parent who observes coaching behavior and acts accordingly?

- Who in your life do you admire?

- Perspective is an important aspect in all facets of life. Who keeps you focused on a "no scoreboard" mentality?

4

NOBODY LIKES WHINERS

ARRIVING AT NORTHWESTERN AND FIGHTING FOR PLAYING TIME

For some reason, I was never really bothered by the fact that I was moving to the suburb of Evanston, Illinois (right outside of Chicago, one of the largest cities in the country) by myself when I was 18 years old. Even after growing up in the close-knit, comfortable town of Brunswick, Maine, I wasn't scared or nervous, and I really was not worried about being homesick. Going off to college was truly a special experience for me, one for which I was ready and eager. I felt as though I'd been sufficiently nurtured by my parents and that I could take on the world. I didn't cry when my parents dropped me off—even though they did. I had no idea I was supposed to!

I was much more focused on and excited about the athletic and academic challenges that lay ahead of me. One of the reasons I liked Northwestern was the two beaches on Lake Michigan that were almost directly on campus. These lakefront views reminded me of Maine's awesome bodies of water in a small but significant way that allowed me to feel very much at home.

I met and quickly bonded with some of the players on the Northwestern team during my visit. The team's best player was Anucha Browne, a girl with a great smile, brilliant sense of humor, and wonderful personality. Connie Erickson was another player who immediately took me under her wing.

The problem I immediately found, however, was that the Northwestern team was guard-heavy—and I was a guard. One mistake I made in the recruiting process was really not asking the correct questions about how I would fit into the team and what my role would be. We didn't have a guard spot open when I was a freshman, and I really had to work very hard just to earn some playing time. I realized, looking back, that Duke would have been a better fit for me, simply because that team needed guards. I think I worried more about the academic part of the equation of where to attend school and did not pay enough attention to the basketball side of it. I ended up paying a price for that and really had to work to differentiate my skills and show that I should be part of the rotation.

Near the end of my freshman season, I earned a starting spot from Coach Annette Lynch. It was the first time in my life that I had been coached by a woman. It never really occurred to me until I got to Northwestern that all of my coaches had been men. I had no problem having men as my mentors and role models; it had always seemed perfectly normal and natural to me.

However, I certainly did not have any problem respecting a woman coach—especially Annette, who had been at the school for three years. Northwestern had only had a women's basketball team since 1975, and the NCAA had only taken over the postseason National Championship tournament the previous year. I really did notice more effects of the Title IX legislation in college, since Northwestern was clearly committed by completely funding many women's teams.

I also was coming to a school that had struggled for years with many of its athletic programs, at least in the major sports. The school's football team had set a record by losing 34 consecutive games—a streak that ended shortly before I arrived there. The men's basketball team was not quite *that* bad, but they certainly were not a contender for the Big Ten championship, either. On the other hand, women's sports at Northwestern were rocking—except, that is, for basketball. We needed to catch up to the level of the softball, volleyball, field hockey, and lacrosse teams. Northwestern is very progressive in supporting all sports, and that was one of the benefits they touted to me and my mother as I was being recruited—how much the school valued women's sports. Within just weeks of starting college, I saw firsthand that it was indeed true.

My biggest personal problem—other than having to fight for playing time for the first time in my life—was that I had lost almost my entire support system. Ever since I began to play in middle school, my parents had always been in the stands, and now they hardly ever saw me play. I also learned that an all-American guard from Maine was really not as exciting at Northwestern as a good guard from Illinois who could steadily generate local interest. I struggled with this issue of consistency until my senior year.

It's funny to look back at that time in my life with the perspective I have gained after so many years of coaching. I now realize how many uninformed choices I made. Though I had an excellent experience at Northwestern overall, I had merely a good, but not great, career there. I made poor choices in friends early on; for example, my best friend that year was a smoker. She was very funny and did not seem to take life seriously, which was an odd choice of a friend for someone like me who had always been very focused. This girl didn't study; instead, she partied and was the type of person I had never seen before. I suppose that's what attracted me to her. I can distinctly recall my mother's reaction on meeting this girl when my parents made their first visit to Northwestern: *Are you kidding me?* She immediately knew we had nothing in common. Our friendship soon fell apart, and I gravitated more to my teammates.

This was a great lesson in knowing that true friendships are indeed a response to values and sharing some common ground. Our perceptions and judgments can often become skewed when we're away from home for the first time, or engaged in any other entirely new experience. We occasionally do things and choose friends based on image, insecurity issues, or fascination rather than something real—like shared interests and a basic level of trust.

A Coaching Change

Another challenge for me in college (one that many players face) came when we changed coaches after my freshman year. Annette left after we had gone 15 and 12 and finished fifth in the Big Ten (a slight drop-off from the previous two seasons). Although I had not become especially close to Annette, I wasn't sure what to think. I was shocked that she was leaving, and I did what kids usually do in that situation: I pulled back and kept my feelings and thoughts to myself. A situation like this is hard; you can't talk to the old coach because she's leaving, and the new coach doesn't know you, so you just don't talk to anybody.

I thought to myself, *This is Northwestern; they have smart people here.* As such, I was confident that the school would hire somebody good to take Annette's place. This was one of the first times I really understood that important people, the people that you enjoy, are all replaceable in some way. Timing simply has a way of ensuring that the change occurs.

I think part of what I went through during this coaching change left me better prepared for the times I have gone through it as a coach. Just because you were not the coach who recruited a particular player does not mean you cannot develop a good relationship with that individual. When I have changed jobs, I have inherited many players on my teams whom I did not recruit, and even though it took extra work, I was able to establish a positive rapport with almost all of those players.

The same concept applies to a business environment. A new boss who enters a given company obviously did not hire the people who now are working for him or her. However, that doesn't mean he or she cannot develop an authentic, effective relationship with them. It also doesn't mean that employees can't like their new boss just as much as (or more than) their old boss.

There was a period of time when transferring to another school was a possibility for me; however, I never considered it very seriously. Sometimes I casually mentioned the idea of transferring when another student-athlete asked how things were going. I thought it would turn into a conversation topic, and I was wondering about it myself and decided to share my thinking.

Instead, this statement had quite the opposite effect: It caused people to separate themselves from me. That period in my life taught me a valuable lesson: Nobody likes whiners. I learned that people genuinely want to hear and talk about positive topics—an incredibly maturing lesson for me. The topic of transferring was not a popular one; other people didn't look upon it positively. The pride factor was too great, and running from a problem seemed immature and needy.

Another lesson I learned from that experience was that if I did move to another school, I really would be running away from a problem, not working to solve it. I would be quitting something I started before I had finished it, and I quickly dropped the idea.

I see a lot of kids transferring from one school to another these days (sometimes more than once), and it continues to bother me. I understand completely that it's incredibly difficult when you don't feel good about a place; however, I still believe it really is an unhelpful and discouraging way to think. It is crucial to stick with the commitments we make, even from an early age. Of course, there are mitigating circumstances from time to time, but there's generally a lot to be said for standing behind the choices we make.

I also knew that the most significant reason I was attending Northwestern had nothing to do with basketball and everything to do with getting a quality education. I really never had any intention of becoming a coach while I was in school, and there were virtually no options available for women to keep playing basketball after they had graduated. Therefore, I knew my education was going to be the most important factor in the kind of career I pursued.

We had one outstanding player on our team, Anucha Browne (now Anucha Brown Sanders), a native of Brooklyn, New York, who won all–Big Ten honors for three consecutive years and was the Big Ten player of the year twice. When Anucha was a senior during my sophomore year, she averaged 30 points a game.

I had lost my starting spot before we went to California to play UCLA and Long Beach State, and I was upset about it. I had been playing out of position as a forward (due to the fact that we had quality guards), and our coach decided he wanted to go with a bigger lineup against those teams. I was shooting baskets by myself after practice a few days later when Anucha came over to me and asked me what I was going to do about it. She was our leader and the personality and center of our team. She was a powerful, smart, honest woman of integrity.

Unfortunately, I didn't realize this at the time, so I told Anucha to shut up and leave me alone. She was a very intimidating woman, standing 6 feet 2 inches tall, with long legs, and when she continued to try to badger me, I tried to push her away. She was trying to motivate me, because she saw it as her role. But I was unhappy with myself, and her interference, though well-intentioned, was personal to me.

No punches were thrown, and before we could try to hit each other, another player, a small guard named Stacy Neal, who came from a town named Beloit, Illinois, had joined the conversation. She jumped on my back with a big bear hug and tried to pull me away from Anucha.

"Are you crazy?" Stacy said, looking at me like I was insane. "She'll kill you!"

Anucha knew that my anger wasn't truly aimed at her, and we became closer after that incident. The coaches had not seen what happened, and nobody really talked about it. It is amazing how conflict brings clarity. After this incident, Anucha and I understood each other on a new level.

My sophomore and junior years were tough for me, because I had never been a reserve player before. I started only six of our 27 games as a junior, but was able to tolerate it early in the year because we were winning. The good times didn't last, however, as we won only 6 of our final 18 games.

By the time I was a senior, I was back in the starting lineup playing guard. That year was really the only good season of my career. I started all 30 games, averaged 12 points a game (almost leading the team), and was named a first-team all–Big Ten all-academic selection—an honor that made me incredibly proud. I worked hard in the classroom and tried to get good grades, and earning that title validated all my hard work.

I was a political science major, and I really did receive an education in politics at Northwestern—in the classroom as well as on the basketball court. It was an extremely liberal education, with a lot of the professors talking about how Marxism and Communism were really perfect society models. I was struck by the passions and convictions they had in their beliefs, given the lives and freedoms they enjoyed in the United States. What they thought sometimes seemed to me to be at odds with the way they lived. I can remember being perplexed about this perceived conundrum or paradox. I enjoyed the classes, but I was also quick to reason through their points of view and look for consistency in thoughts and actions.

While I was motivated for every game as a senior, the game I looked forward to the most that season was when we hosted Tennessee. The Volunteers were coached then, as they are now, by Pat Summit, who is a legend of women's basketball. However, Pat didn't know that in addition to wanting to win against her team, I had another reason for feeling especially stimulated for that game: I was mad at her for not recruiting me out of high school.

That was my passion and fighter mentality kicking in again. I had been a good player in high school, voted one of the top 40 seniors in the country. So why, I wondered, hadn't I been good enough for Pat to recruit? Not that I would have gone to Tennessee, but I still wanted to show her she had made a mistake. I scored 20 points, which was a good game for me; however, we still lost by three. Funny how coaches can motivate even opponents sometimes.

My First (Bittersweet) Taste of the NCAA Tournament

We won 20 games that year, and made our only appearance in the NCAA Tournament—the first time Northwestern had qualified for the tournament in five years. We beat Kansas State at home in overtime the first game. That win moved us into the second round at Louisiana Tech. We had six seniors on the team, and we were happy and playing well.

However, during practice the day before the game, I landed on another player's foot and badly sprained my ankle. I kept my ankle in an ice bucket the night before, trying to get the swelling down. It was black and purple and all kinds of ugly colors. I didn't know if I would be able to play or not.

I certainly wouldn't have thought twice about not playing if this had just been a regular season game. But there was no way I was going to miss this game. My ankle was taped so heavily it almost looked like it was in a cast, but I played. My assignment was to guard Teresa Weatherspoon, one of the best players in the country—something that would have been hard enough on a healthy ankle. We also were playing in a very hostile environment in Rustin, Louisiana; at one point, I was actually hit by a coin thrown out of the stands when I was getting ready to shoot a free throw.

We lost the game by about 20 points. Although I was in excruciating physical pain afterward because of my ankle, the other seniors and I were also in tremendous emotional pain. We knew we had played our last game, and everyone was crying. My ankle was throbbing, and my career was over.

The off-the-court lessons at Northwestern were profound. Almost all of the talk at the fraternity parties at Northwestern was about what you were going to do after you graduated—and it seemed as though everyone I talked to was planning to go to either medical school or law school. At age 21, these people seemed to have their entire lives mapped out. They talked openly about how they were going to be a judge, or a senator, or maybe an actor because Northwestern had such a great theater department.

As for me, I really had no idea; so I just told people I was going to go to law school. Though this wasn't really a passion for me, it was an easy and convenient thing to say that brought no arguments. My college boyfriend, Tim Joranko, had gone on from Northwestern to Harvard Law School and was a practicing attorney in Chicago by that time.

Northwestern has a great alumni base, and I was hired as an intern at one of the most prestigious law firms in downtown Chicago (Winston and Strawn) the summer between my junior and senior years.

Tim and I had met and begun dating during the spring of my freshman year, and we remained together throughout college. Tim taught me about life and compassion and how to think and expand my academic limits. He was a deep thinker, very bright, with an innate desire to help others. We argued about philosophical issues, but he taught me how to think for myself and to be my own person. We played one-on-one basketball for hours and he pushed me to be the best I could be in all phases of my life.

I didn't realize until years later that while there was a tremendous upside to having a long-term boyfriend in college, there were also some drawbacks to dating the same person that whole time, even as great as Tim was. I see now that I missed out on so much, and I wouldn't recommend that other young people get involved in such a serious, long-term relationship at that stage in their lives. It wasn't entirely healthy for either one of us to become so dependent on each other; in fact, it proved to be the reason that we separated. I was simply too young, without many comparative life experiences to help develop further emotional security.

Though Tim and I were very much in love, we were apart for three years when he was at Harvard. I learned during this time how important it is to engage in your campus community and make sure you allow yourself to date or do other fun activities with your classmates. I allowed myself to be a little more isolated, and I certainly would encourage my daughter and son to just make certain that they take part in the full collegiate life—dating, social, academic, and other experiences. I spent a lot of time commuting back and forth from Northwestern to Harvard. While that time was, of course, special, it also took me away from many other opportunities to grow.

One year our team decided to attend the Final Four as fans. We went as a group for a kind of team-building exercise. I chose to go spend the weekend with Tim and his family at his home in Albion, Michigan, instead. I was the only member of my team not to participate in that trip to the Final Four, and I regret it to this day. I implore every young person who has the chance to attend college to make wise choices and get as full an experience as possible when you're there. You won't get another opportunity to live these years.

Tim and I were still dating exclusively when I graduated, and he had moved back to Chicago to begin his law career. I knew I was staying in Chicago, at least for the time being, but that was all I knew.

Coach P instructing Jasmine Thomas (number 5) during the 2010 ACC Championship Game against NC State in Greensboro, North Carolina. Duke won the game 70 to 60 to win its first ACC Championship under Joanne P. McCallie.
Source: Duke Photography

CHAPTER 4 QUESTIONS

- It is the people who are positive in life who prosper. Are *you* a positive person?
- What friendships do you have in your life? Do these friendships make you better?
- Are you authentic in your life? Are the people around you authentic?
- Change is a natural force in life. Are you open to change?
- Conflict exists in our professional and personal lives. Are you comfortable facing it?
- Can you identify consistency in the actions of the important people in your life?

5

Money Alone
Won't Make
You Happy

WHAT AM I GOING TO DO WITH MY LIFE?

I really did not have a backup career plan after I ruled out law school. I envied my classmates who knew exactly what they wanted to do after graduation, who had a passion to pursue a career in medicine, or law, or business. I had yet to find my passion.

Because Tim was going to be living and working in Chicago, all I knew was that I wanted to stay there. With Northwestern's help, I was able to land an interview with a telecommunications company, and the executive hired me on the spot. I was so thankful to have a job and something to do that I didn't even realize until I showed up for my first day of work that it was in sales.

The office was at 100 South Wacker in downtown Chicago—and all of a sudden, I was a city girl. About the only thing I did that reflected my small-town background was refuse to pay to park my old cherry-red Volvo every day when I went to work. This meant I had to find a spot on the street, usually a pretty good distance away from the office, and walk through the snow and cold every morning to save a few dollars.

While my motivation to save money was the reason I didn't want to pay to park, I had another incentive to work hard at my job, even though I didn't enjoy it very much and didn't know how successful I would be. When I showed up for my first day of work, the manager showed me a quota board; my name was on the bottom, below all of the other sales representatives.

"You need to get to the top," the manager told me.

As a competitive individual, that was all I needed to hear. Whatever it took, whatever I had to do to succeed, I had my goal right in front of me. I looked at the quota board every day, and was constantly working to ensure that my name would one day be the one on top.

It took a little while, but I did it. I was making good money, wearing nice clothes, and felt satisfied that I was doing a good job and that my work was appreciated. Still, there was something missing in my life—a passion for what I was doing and a true overall happiness and sense of excitement about my future.

For the first time in my life, I was hit by the realization that money alone was not enough to make me happy. Even though I had been working at this job for less than a year, I knew I wasn't fulfilled, and I also knew that there was no way I could see myself doing this job for the rest of my life. I knew some classmates who thought happiness came from getting a good job and making a lot of money, but that didn't happen in my case, and I honestly don't think it happens for a lot of people. In addition to lacking real a passion for what I was doing, I didn't see any purpose in my life. I was lonely, scared, and confused about what to do next.

I know I am not the first woman (or man, for that matter) to experience that feeling. I am sure that part of this frustration came from the fact that I was questioning my relationship with Tim around this time as well. Since we had been completely devoted to each other for almost five years, this consternation was incredibly painful.

Most of our friends just assumed we would be married after staying together for so many years, especially considering the fact that we had survived a long-distance relationship while Tim was at Harvard Law School. Even though I loved him very much, I knew in my heart we were not ready for the next step. And if we were not going to be married, what would our relationship's future be?

I knew the answer, deep down: The upsetting yet obvious fact was that our relationship didn't have a future.

We had spent almost five years together, and our breakup was very difficult and distressing. Tim was headed to Guatemala to work for the Peace Corps within six months, and I was preparing to leave Chicago for a graduate assistant position in women's basketball. I learned from this situation that while change can be incredibly trying at times, it also brings clarity. Tim had a passion to work in the Peace Corps that he hadn't entirely embraced; in fact, we had been holding each other back a little. Nobody wants to change, but ironically, our breakup gave both of us the freedom to follow our life's passions.

FOLLOWING A PASSION: MY RETURN TO BASKETBALL

I had occasionally gone back to Northwestern to visit some friends on the basketball team and watch practices while working at my sales job. Breaking up with Tim had given me the strength to try to do something else, to make a change in my life—and as it had been ever since I became serious about the sport, I turned back to basketball for my salvation and direction.

I was tired of the cold weather, and the long walks through the rough Chicago winters from my free parking spot to the office seemed to be taking longer and longer. So I did what seemed to make the most sense to me: to get out of Chicago and find someplace a lot warmer. It also made sense to me that I should go back to school and pursue an MBA degree, which I knew would make me more qualified for any job I decided to try in the future.

The NCAA publishes a guide each year that lists all of the member schools. One day at a Northwestern practice, I was talking about my plan to get my MBA when one of the assistant coaches flipped me a copy of the book. I took it home and contacted every warm-weather school I could find that had an MBA program.

Even though I had made good money working at the sales job, and had saved it well, I wanted to see if I could land a job as a graduate assistant coach for the women's basketball team; this way, I would be paid to attend the two-year graduate school program. So, I had to find (1) a warm-weather school, (2) one that needed a grad assistant, and (3) that also offered an MBA.

Luckily, I had some choices, and I narrowed my final decision down to two schools: Vanderbilt and Auburn. I knew I needed to talk personally with the two head coaches—Phil Lee at Vanderbilt and Joe Ciampi at Auburn—but I also made the conscious decision that I did not want to visit either school before I made the final choice if I were offered either position.

The reason was obvious to me: I knew I would love Vanderbilt, as well as Nashville's big city feel and exciting environment. I knew

Auburn was a much more rural school, and I didn't want my decision to be based solely on which area I liked the best. I knew this was a bold decision, but I also believed in my heart it was the only way to make a choice. If I went to both schools before deciding, I would be picking a school because of the level of comfort I felt rather than the depth of what the coach and school could offer me professionally.

Both schools offered good programs. Auburn had qualified for the Final Four, which was in Tacoma, Washington, in 1988. Vanderbilt had failed to make the NCAA Tournament after going the previous two years; however, it turned out Phil was going to Tacoma that year, anyway. So I made arrangements to fly to Tacoma, on my own dime, to talk with both coaches.

I had a great interview with Phil. He was doing a really good job of selling the school, and he talked about how it would be the perfect fit for me after having gone to another great academic school like Northwestern. My mother was right on board as well, continuing her philosophy of trying to make sure I got the best possible education and value for my dollar.

The Auburn interview with Joe was much different. He invited me to join the team at a dinner the night before the National Championship game at the Final Four, and I had to find the restaurant on my own, in the rain, 40 miles outside of Tacoma. Joe really did not try to recruit me; it was actually a very awkward environment. I was sitting with the team, next to a vice president of the school. I didn't know anybody in the room, and I felt really out of place.

Joe did talk to me later, but the basic message he delivered was, "If you want to come, come; but I'm going to need to know soon." That was it. The two coaches had very different styles, but I liked both of them.

It would seem on the surface as though it would make the most sense for me to go to Vanderbilt. That was where my mother wanted me to go. My father, however, was more open-minded. He wanted me to go where I could learn the most about basketball, even though at the moment my whole motivation in becoming a grad assistant was so I would not have to pay to get my MBA.

My decision really was driven by the fact that I had not been to a Final Four before and had not seen women's basketball played at the highest level. Auburn had been there, and I thought the team had a good chance of continuing to play at that high level. Even though Vanderbilt had a good team with a good program, and it was a Southeastern Conference school, it was not quite at that level.

Therefore, my choice, which can serve as a lesson for every young person who finds him- or herself in a similar situation, boiled down to a "best-person" decision. I needed to learn, and I thought Joe Ciampi would be the better teacher—something I was able to see in him as he coached those games in Tacoma. It's unfortunate that many young people today often do not know how to evaluate others because of sinking communication skills—a result of all our new and wonderful modern technology. I was looking for the person who I thought would help me learn the most, and my gut told me that person was Joe, despite his unorthodox interview technique.

My competitive nature came through again in my efforts to make the decision about where to go. I had always wanted to be the best player I could be, and I was the type of player who operated well under pressure; the more intense the competition, the better I played.

Joe emphasized this approach. He had come from West Point and was a very matter-of-fact coach and individual. He told me that if I wanted to see women's basketball at the highest level possible, I would come to Auburn. It was a much different style of recruiting, but Joe could tell what would work for him and for me.

Without too much debate, I decided to go to Auburn. I was also convinced that I had found a true mentor in Joe Ciampi.

Coach P with the 2011 Duke Women's Basketball team following a 66 to 58 win against the University of North Carolina on February 27, 2011, at Cameron Indoor Stadium. The win clinched a share of the 2011 ACC Regular Season Championship and was Senior Day for the Class of 2011.
Source: Duke Photography

CHAPTER 5 QUESTIONS

- What is your quota board in your life? Where do you want to be in nine months?
- Happiness is found in different places for different people. What makes you happy? Is money driving your passion?
- When have you found clarity through change in your life? What happened during the time of transition to allow clarity?
- How do you make career decisions in your life? What is most important to you when making these decisions?

6

NEVER BE AFRAID TO TRY SOMETHING AND MAKE A MISTAKE

MAKING A COMMITMENT AND STICKING WITH IT

I packed my red Volvo and headed south from Chicago. I was excited, but also nervous and unsure of myself. As I pulled into the town in rural Alabama, passing farms and cows and a run-down bar, I began to cry. What had I done? Had I made the greatest mistake of my life? What kind of place had I come to?

I knew in my heart why I had picked Auburn, and I knew the only reason I was there was because of my decision not to visit either school before I made my choice. There was no question that if I had made those two visits I would have picked Vanderbilt. The way in which I decided could really be taught in corporate boardrooms, since my decision was about people—and putting vision before circumstance. Life is about interaction with others, how you motivate yourself and those around you, and how you are going to develop. That's much more important than what a place looks like. I'm fascinated I had this view even at a very young age and after living in Chicago. It seems as though I received some really good lessons about what is important, since I knew I didn't need to see either school and was instead committed to the belief that having a mentor was the important thing.

As with any decision, you never know what would have happened had you made the opposite decision. I didn't want to think about that, however, no matter how unhappy I was during my first year at Auburn.

It didn't seem as though a day went by that year that I did not cry at least once. I was miserable. I was homesick. Yet when I talked to my parents, they expressed somewhat of a "tough love" attitude: *You made the choice; now deal with it.* I don't know if I expected them to react differently, but they certainly never gave me the option of coming home if I wanted. I questioned whether I was cut out for coaching, and the answer was almost always no.

I knew that deep down by this point in my life that if I made a commitment, I was going to see it through. This "commitment" philosophy is really important to growing and understanding what real ownership means. I find that many of today's athletes sometimes react in an impetuous way. It seems as though the minute something does not work out for them, they want to leave and go someplace else. They also seem to get their parents' approval to do it far too frequently, which amazes me.

My parents did not support my desire to flee. They were clear about their opinion that I needed to fight through whatever challenged me. There was just no way I was going anywhere. Though incredibly difficult, of course, it's always fulfilling to work through adversity, and good parents know that they can't take those challenges away from kids. It was a difficult year, but I was determined to get through it—and my parents' resolve was particularly important.

I don't know what my parents would have said or done had I told them I was going to leave Auburn and come home, but I know they would have been very upset with me for not finishing something I chose to start.

This is one way in which parents choose to lead—or not. Without this kind of guidance, young people can find themselves adrift and left to sort through their whims and feelings. Reason over emotion can work far better in life, but a parent must be willing to step forward and lead his or her child through the hard times.

Working through a new period of time in my life is what made me grow, toughen, and eventually mature. Staying the course while being able to "turn the page" daily and sort through what my boss expected was an invaluable time of growth. Genuine expertise and knowledge is a long-term project. Staying focused is so important.

Getting through that first year at Auburn was one of the hardest things I have ever done; it also felt like one of the longest years of my life. I knew nobody. I shared an apartment with an athletic trainer, but she was engaged and often gone. I signed up for tennis lessons and joined a karate group and a bike club. I did anything and everything I could to stay busy and try to keep from being so lonely.

Coaching seemed so selfless to me, and the kids seemed to need so much, both on and off the court. Nothing made sense to me that entire year. Going to school and working did not leave me with a lot of free time. Joe was a very demanding boss; he quickly realized that even though I had played Division I basketball at a good school, I still had a lot to learn. I found out there was a significant difference between being a player and becoming an experienced and successful coach.

Fortunately for me, Joe started teaching me how to be a coach from day one. He showed no elitism; my desk was right there in his office. It was my job to do all of the work that nobody else wanted to do, but that was how I learned. Coaching is definitely a learned craft, and requires that people develop a skill set. So many try to carry their playing days into coaching, wearing them as a badge of knowledge, and often struggle in the transition. But coaching is different than playing; it is truly a profession.

My days began at 5:30 AM for the bike club rides, which went until 7:00 AM. My classes started at 8:00 and were all in the morning. From 12:30 to 3:00, I attended team practice. I did office work until 6:00, ate dinner, and then studied and did homework until I went to bed at 11:30 PM. That was my schedule for two years straight, six days a week. I was lucky if I had one day a week off for that entire year.

Joe was very organized and had a lot of structure in his program, which I am sure came from his military background and the time he spent coaching at West Point. As the daughter of a Navy pilot, I embraced that philosophy and observed that it was very successful for the student-athletes.

I knew how to listen and show respect and be careful with assumptions and random ideas. I learned very quickly that my actions spoke louder than words. To this day, I am concerned when someone claims to be loyal or to support me. Usually those are the types who do not recognize that their actions speak the most. It doesn't do much to tell someone that you're loyal. What matters is to show it on a daily basis.

One thing that helped me learn and develop as a coach under Joe was a personal philosophy that I had carried with me since I was young: I never hesitated to try something and make a mistake. A high school English teacher once told me that one of my best attributes was that I was never afraid to be wrong—and she was right. Of course, I like being right a lot more than I like being wrong; however, I quickly learned that making mistakes provides the opportunity to learn and truly improve in countless ways. The openness to err—and therefore to get better—often sends you in a better direction when looking for a solution.

During that first year, I was so busy and making so many adjustments in my life that it still hadn't hit me that I had found my life's passion in coaching. I was focused on getting my MBA and learning about coaching; therefore, it took a while to sink in that I was doing what I would likely be doing the rest of my life.

We had a good team, and came into the season with a lot of incentive. Auburn had been 14 points ahead of Louisiana Tech in the National Championship game in 1988, but could only watch as that lead disappeared when Louisiana Tech came back and claimed a 56 to 54 win, for the national title. It was the team's third loss in 35 games during the season—an unbelievable record.

If possible, Auburn was even better in the 1988–1989 season. We did not lose a game until March (to Tennessee), and once again reached the NCAA Final Four—facing semifinal opponent Louisiana Tech. We got our revenge from the previous year's loss, moving into the title game for the second year in a row. But Tennessee was waiting for us, and once again, the game did not go our way. We had to settle for a runner-up finish for the second consecutive year.

THINGS BEGIN TO MAKE SENSE

By the start of my second year at Auburn, I knew I had made the right choice in where to go to school—and the reason for this was Joe. He had been right; working there had allowed me to see basketball at the highest level. It was becoming increasingly clear to me what coaching was all about, and I could see myself making progress as a coach. Things suddenly began to make sense, and I was forming relationships to the point where I could see the value and fun of developing young folks daily.

What convinced me that I could coach actually did not happen on the court, however, but instead took place on a bus.

Our point guard that year was Chantel Tremitiere, a junior with a very creative and precocious personality. My job at Auburn included working with the point guards, so I took on a mentoring role with her. As I was only a couple of years older than our players, I was more of a sister to them than an authority figure. This made developing that healthy coach/player relationship a bit tricky at times.

Though Chantel was a good player, I didn't think she was playing as well as she could, nor was she acting like the leader a point guard really needs to be. We were on the bus one day, and I told her to slide over to make room for me to sit with her. She refused. It was the action of a typical arrogant kid trying to provoke me. She looked at me, shrugged, and did not move. She was challenging the coach and being a pain in the rear for no apparent reason. I got in her face and yelled at her, and really let her have it. We didn't come to blows, but it was incredibly close.

Whether that was the spark she needed or not, the incident seemed to incite a bond between us. Conflict and confrontation in even the simplest way over the silliest circumstances can bring clarity to a situation like nothing else. In this way, reaffirming boundaries is crucial. I believe that seizing an authentic moment like this is the key. As a result of that interaction, Chantel became a better player and led us back to the Final Four. We also gained a spot in the National Championship game for the third consecutive year, an amazing feat for a team with only one returning starter. Once more, however, the title was not meant to be ours, even though Chantel scored a career-high 17 points. We may have lost that game, but I was so proud of her growth throughout the year. She got us back to the title game.

More important than winning or losing that championship for me was the transformation I made as a person that year. I started to understand coaching. Watching Chantel and some of the other players helped me realize that I could help develop people by working as a coach. I could try to make them better basketball players, true, but more important, I could try to make them better people. I knew I could challenge them mentally and make them think. It was exciting to see their eyes when a given topic I discussed registered in their brains and began to make sense to them.

Working with Joe made me better at the X's and O's—the basic knowledge of how to coach, how to watch film, and what to look for that would help create a winning game plan. After being so lost and alone those first months in Auburn, I felt as though my life was starting to fall in place.

I also achieved a great feat off the court by receiving my MBA. My parents came down from Maine for graduation—the first time they had ever been to the campus. I still like to joke with them about this fact. It was a special time to share my Auburn world with them. I was very proud of that MBA and the time it took to make it all work.

However, I didn't really have to think about that when Joe offered me a job as a full-time assistant coach. Over the two years of working as a graduate assistant, I had about gone through all of the money I had saved from my job in Chicago, so it was going to be nice to actually earn a paycheck again.

The other reason I was smiling a lot more, however, had to do with a man named John McCallie who had suddenly come into my life.

One of my favorite teachers at Auburn was a big Hungarian man named Tibor Machan, who taught philosophy. It was a difficult class, but one I really enjoyed. One night some friends and I were out at dinner, and I saw him in the restaurant, so I walked up to say hello. He introduced me to the man he was having dinner with—John McCallie. It turned out John was working on his PhD in economics. It was a low-key meeting, and after a couple of minutes, I rejoined my friends and didn't think anything more about it.

After dinner, my group went to hang out at another place—a beat-up bar called The Supper Club that stayed open until 4:00 AM. My friend Kim and I were talking and saw John walk in the front door.

"Look, there's that guy we just met," Kim said. John saw us and came over, and we began talking again. It turned out he had found out where we were going and followed us there. After talking for a while, John asked if I played tennis, and we agreed to meet and play the next night at 9:30 PM. People around Auburn didn't do much physical activity earlier in the day because it was simply too hot, so nighttime tennis was popular and a lot of fun.

However, I began to get a little worried as it got closer to the time we were to meet. I considered myself pretty good athletically, and I wondered what would happen if I actually beat John. I decided I didn't want to do that, but I also didn't want it to look like I was letting him win. A thousand thoughts ran through my head regarding how I should play, act, or be on that tennis court.

It turned out I didn't have anything to worry about. John smoked me 6–0, 6–0 in 15 minutes without really trying. He played as he might have played with his brothers, but he was still such a gentleman. I couldn't return his serve or really do anything. I looked like the most unathletic human being ever.

Luckily, my lack of prowess during that match didn't discourage him. We left the tennis court and went to dinner, and for whatever reason, we just hit it off. It was like he instantly became my best friend in the world, and has stayed that way for 20 years of marriage.

I didn't really know a lot about John's background. I learned he was part of a large family that came from Chattanooga and that he had received his undergrad degree at North Carolina and his master's at Tennessee. I knew he was a few years older than me, but it wasn't anything that really concerned me. His athleticism, energy, and sense of life and adventure were very apparent.

We began to hang around together a lot, and one day something came up and I casually asked him how old he was. I was 24 at the time. He told me to guess, and I think I said, "About 30." He said I was "close," and we moved on to talk about something else.

I didn't think about it as we began to date pretty seriously until one day several months later when he showed me his driver's license. I learned he was 39 years old—15 years older than me. He had never lied to me about his age, and didn't hide it, but he had not told me how old he was, either. It was interesting dating dynamics indeed, stunning to me at the time, but totally insignificant overall. Did age really matter? I suppose we were about to find out.

Even though I was surprised, his age didn't really bother me. I had gotten to know John pretty well by then. I knew that I genuinely liked him and that the difference in our ages should not become a reason we could not see each other if we really enjoyed each other.

My family was concerned with the age difference, however—especially when John and I decided we wanted to get married. My point of view on the issue is simple. Love is a response to values. I was more in love with John, regardless of his age, because of his values than I could possibly have been with a 24-year-old who did not share my philosophy and opinions about life.

I had really gotten to know the sense of life that John possessed, and how we saw eye-to-eye on most matters. He really loved my career and supported my desire to be a coach, and I knew there were many times when he would have loved to change places with me and become a coach while I would become the college professor. Our career reciprocity was very high, and we each thoroughly enjoyed the other's passion for teaching.

The first serious challenge I faced in our relationship came when John took a job teaching at the University of Alabama in Birmingham. I was coaching at Auburn, and it was not going to be easy for either one of us to commute from one city to another. John had an aunt and uncle who lived in Birmingham, so he stayed with them while he was teaching in the middle of the week.

A NEARLY FATAL MISTAKE

John and I rented a house in Dadesville, Alabama, which made it a little easier for John to commute. It was an easy drive for me, and I became a little overconfident after making the drive every day, so I could drive without concentrating totally when I was behind the wheel.

That was nearly a fatal mistake.

I didn't have a book on tape to listen to while I was driving to work one morning, so I decided to catch up on the latest news by flipping the pages of the new issue of *Time* magazine while I was driving. I just thought it would be a productive use of my time; I simply wasn't thinking about the potentially deadly consequences.

It was another example of how young and truly inexperienced I still was. I don't know why I thought I could put the magazine down on the passenger seat and just flip through the pages, glancing up and down while I was driving, but that's what I did. Then, suddenly, I looked up to find that my car, a Ford Escort, was headed off the road.

I missed a curve, and the car started going out of control. All I could see in front of me were trees, and I was certain I was going to hit one. The next thing I knew, the car flipped upside down. I counted the revolutions, three, before it finally came to rest on the roof—somehow without hitting a tree. I was still strapped in my seat belt (the one good decision I made that morning), and as I was trying to come to grips with what had happened and the fact that I was still alive, I began to smell gas.

A new level of panic set in. I had survived the accident, but what would happen if the gas tank suddenly caught fire and the car burst into flames? I was trapped, trying desperately to get out of my seat belt (remember, I was upside down in the car, staring at the sky). One advantage I did have was that the windows were manual windows and not automatic, and I was able to reach the door and roll the window down. I finally squirmed out of my seat belt and climbed out.

If there had been automatic windows in the car there is no way I could have gotten out, because I never would have been able to break the window. I don't know how long I would have been trapped there. The car was quite a way off the road, in a ditch, and mostly out of sight.

As I climbed out, I could tell the car had also gone down a hill in addition to just going off the road, and I was several feet below street level. I could have been hidden among the trees for who knows how long before somebody would have spotted me.

I got far enough away from the car that I knew I would be okay even if it burst into flames, and then tried to see how badly I was hurt. Amazingly, the only blood I saw was running down my leg from where I had cut my knee.

I felt disoriented because of the wreck, and the fact that it was a very hot day didn't help matters. I didn't know exactly where I was; and of course, there were no cell phones at that time. I had to walk about a half mile until I found an old, dilapidated trailer. The people who came to the door were the most fascinating, caring people I had ever met in my life. They led me into their kitchen, gave me their phone, and asked who I needed to call.

Since John was two hours away in Birmingham, the first person I called was Joe. I completely broke down when he got on the phone, and he immediately drove out and picked me up. The experience stayed with me for a long time; it made me shaky when I got back behind the wheel, and I never again tried that stunt of reading a magazine while I was driving.

Once I was certain I was okay, my next reaction was how embarrassed I was about what had happened. I knew there was nobody to blame but myself. I also knew that my life had been spared for a reason . . . perhaps so I could use my experiences to send a message to others about how quickly something like that can happen.

Firsthand experience is the best teacher in any situation, but especially in moments like that. Young people in particular think they are invincible and that nothing can ever happen to them. My daughter, Maddie, knows this story, and I have tried to let her and her friends know that this is why I am so concerned when one of them gets behind the wheel of a car. It is amazing how life can change in a split second. Experiencing this firsthand changes you forever.

On a positive note, John and I were married in the summer of 1991, and we moved to Auburn because his schedule made it easier for him to commute than would have been the case for me. I was putting in long hours as a full-time assistant coach, especially during the season, and we made the decision that was best for us together.

We talked a lot about our career goals, both before and after we were married. John had always shown tremendous interest and support for everything I did. He loved women's basketball, in part, I think, because his mother had been the starting point guard while she was a student at Tennessee-Chattanooga. He was fascinated by the sport and also by coaching. I don't know when I made a conscious decision that I wanted to someday become a head coach, but it soon became obvious that this was the plan. I didn't know long it would take or where I would go; these were questions that we could not answer at the time.

In order for a marriage to be successful when both partners have jobs (that they enjoy), communication is truly the most essential element. John and I both knew how important our respective careers were to one another. He was always eager to help me pursue any opportunity I wanted as it came along.

I continued to learn a great deal about coaching from Joe in my two years as his regular assistant. We still had a good team during the 1990–1991 season; we fell just short of making a fourth consecutive trip to the Final Four and lost in the Elite Eight. The next year was a down year; although we still finished above .500, we failed to make the NCAA Tournament.

That year was extremely disappointing, and I really felt I had let Joe down. Having a sense of ownership, integrity, and responsibility came naturally to me; for that reason, I always tended to blame myself when things did not work out well. This sense of responsibility was as indispensable for me as an assistant as it has been as a head coach.

Joe was a demanding boss; he never sugarcoated anything. His military background enabled him to haul off on his assistants when he thought it was needed, and I was okay with that. I never whined about it, as some others did. It simply came down to a fundamental principle: Joe had given me the opportunity to come to Auburn, and I was not going to forget that or change my opinion about him. He was the man who gave me the job. The principle of commitment that he instilled in me is one that I hold very dearly—and the fact that he also taught me how to coach was equally incredible.

Joe helped me mature and grow as a coach in many ways, but he may not have realized how he also motivated me with some subtle little digs. He knew I wanted to be a head coach and that I had applied for one job, at Northern Arizona, and that I wanted it all—a great marriage, a great job, kids.

It was very clear to me that coaching was a difficult profession, and I did wonder about how (and sometimes even if) I could do it. But Joe was a very practical man—indeed, a visionary—and part of my motivation to succeed came from the fact that he told me I could *not* have it all. He warned me that I would eventually have to make choices and that either my marriage or my job was going to suffer. I was determined to prove him wrong.

One day in the spring of 1992, I found out that Debbie Leonard was leaving as the head coach at Duke after a long and successful career. Debbie had been the coach who had recruited me out of high school. I had never gotten Duke totally out of my system and flirted with the idea that I should apply for the job.

Joe, of course, was very doubtful about this, and encouraged me to be realistic. He told me they would only consider candidates with head coaching experience. "You can't get that job," he told me. I realized Joe probably was right and I did not send anything to the school, unsure of what they were looking for in coaching candidates.

At around the same time, the head coaching job at the University of Maine, in my home state, opened. I was not going to let this possibility go by without at least finding out about it. Just as I was getting my information together to send to the search committee, they called and asked if I would be interested in the job.

I was, of course; however, there were many factors involved in making this decision. The most important of these had to do with John and his career. Luckily for me, I married an adventurer; John loves the outdoors, and the thought of moving to Maine excited him. He was convinced he could get a teaching position there, so when the University of Maine offered me the coaching job, John was 100 percent in agreement that I should take it. It was an incredibly exciting time for us as a young, aspiring couple.

So, at the age of 26, with only two years as a full-time assistant coach on my resume, I became the head coach at the University of Maine—unaware at the time that I was the youngest head coach in Division I.

Joe just rolled his eyes when I told him the news; however, I could tell he was very proud. It was the third consecutive year he was losing an assistant to a head coaching position, which I think amazed him, even though he was always trying to prepare his assistants to become head coaches. Joe was always fair and firm, and I knew that he wasn't happy to see me go. His program had consistently been taking hits, and I think he was more concerned about that than about whether I was truly qualified to be a head coach.

Even if I had no idea what I was doing, I certainly was not going to admit that to him. There was no looking back now. Our Maine adventure had begun.

Coach P with husband John in Greensboro, North Carolina, following the 2010 ACC Championship Game against North Carolina State on March 7, 2010. The 2010 ACC Championship was the first ACC Championship for Coach P at Duke, as well as her fourth conference championship from four different conferences.
Source: Duke Photography

CHAPTER 6 QUESTIONS

- Throughout the adventures and changes in your life, where have you been able to challenge yourself?
- It is sometimes easier to quit—but not as rewarding—when faced with difficult situations. What difficult situations have you battled through in your life?
- Can you handle conflict with people in your life and make it productive?
- Costly mistakes occur at times in our lives. How do you handle them?
- Has there been a time in your life when conflicts have helped a relationship?

7

SEEK OUT MENTORS

THERE IS NO SUBSTITUTE FOR EXPERIENCE

WHY THE SCOREBOARD IS IRRELEVANT: PLAY THE GAME TO ATTACK AND COMPETE

Accepting the job as the head coach at Maine was the easy step. However, it wasn't very long after making the decision that fear and doubt began to creep into my mind.

I am certain I am not the first woman (or man, for that matter), who has applied to become the boss, knows she is qualified and prepared for the job, then gets the job and wonders . . . what do I do now?

That was exactly the situation I faced as John and I packed up and moved from Auburn to Orono, Maine, in the summer of 1992.

It was reassuring to go home to a state I knew and loved, and to a place where I would be surrounded by friends and family. Support was never the issue; the question I kept asking myself was "How good of a coach can I be?" Though I was happy to know many more people, this familiarity created somewhat of a daily microscope, as well as a lot of internal pressure. I wanted to show everyone what a good job I could do for all of the people who had supported me throughout my playing career.

Empowering others through coaching is the most exciting thing I've ever done. I believe in developing a clear program philosophy, changing the culture where necessary, and establishing consistency while promoting the concept of team power through an "all are one" commitment. I believe—admittedly, somewhat naively—that if you work your tail off and do the best you can do, great things can happen. Change can occur. My greatest strength is my ability to motivate— to lead with passionate reason and great attention to detail while connecting the whole through common understanding and caring, thus believing that anything is possible if we capitalize on the collective power of the whole.

As the coach or leader of any team, your philosophy has to be shared and understood by other members. It's not always easy to get everybody on the same page, because people are products of their own experiences. As an example, you could have issues quietly challenging members of your team and staff. People's inability to take responsibility for themselves is often tracked to a problematic situation where somebody else broke their trust. There is a need in management to understand your people and where they come from. During my early days as a head coach, I struggled with the pace at which folks learned my philosophy; I wanted them all to "get it" sooner rather than later.

Though I was the leader in name, it was hard to clearly express my philosophy to my players and employees. However, it was necessary for me to do so in order to lead through purpose. I knew I was ultimately the one responsible for what happened, and I took that responsibility very seriously. I cared so deeply about every detail, and yet still made so many (incredibly frustrating) mistakes along the way. I learned that sometimes the leader has to override people who don't get it; at the same time, I also had to learn to be patient with those who took more time to learn.

I was in a vulnerable spot as a new leader because my techniques and my thinking weren't proven yet in my current position as a 26-year-old new head coach. That put me in a difficult spot, which tends to be something all new leaders share.

One of the many misconceptions I think people have about coaching is that a coach is only as good as, or motivated by, his or her team's record. People think the coach is happy when the team wins and upset when the team loses. Yet most coaches are generally process-driven, and coaching really goes much deeper than the simple results of a single game. The outcomes are felt deeply, yet the everyday mentality keeps the coach very much in the moment with the team and staff.

I love coaching in games; I love the game strategy and time and score situations. I also love practices, because it is all about the teaching aspect; it's our time to focus on what both individual players and the team as a whole need to do to get better. You measure success by that improvement, and nobody is keeping score relative to this process of growth. You have to make certain that people are "thinking right" in addition to technical strategy. That is one of my core teaching principles.

Games are always interesting to me, since this is where the act of competing together for a shared goal and general betterment comes in. Everybody is in the same bunker during games; however, coaches end up taking on a different role. At practice, I am a taskmaster. In a game, I am the motivator, trying to get us to rally from any situation. I think of myself as a person with strong communication and leadership skills who *became* a coach, not just a person who happens to coach basketball. I mainly work to empower others, and I choose to do this through basketball. I don't embrace a scoreboard mentality, but rather a pursuit of excellence through this process. I—along with my team—play the game to compete. I like to say, "Anytime, anyplace, anywhere, and under any conditions, we attack dangerously."

In fact, the best games are the ones where the scoreboard is irrelevant. It's part of the process. If I have a great team, the players are not interested in looking at the scoreboard; they already know how they are doing. I learned this approach at Michigan State. I had started to develop it at Maine, but didn't label it until later. Great coaches are all about the process, not about the outcome. Since I started my head coaching career with nine straight losses, it was natural for me to concentrate more heavily on process than on being an outcome-driven coach. At the time, it was truly a matter of survival. Things might not have gone exactly the way we wanted; however, enduring that 0 and 9 start really taught me how to frame my thinking and motivation to drive the team forward.

Unfortunately, our first results were not good. Everything that could possibly have gone wrong did.

We lost our first game on the road to Boston College; then we came home to play Florida International. The assistant coaches forgot to put the starters in the scorebook, which cost us a two-shot technical foul. So we were behind 2 to 0 before the game even started, and we lost again. That was a potent example of our staff's inexperience—not to mention the overall failure to communicate by everyone involved.

More losses followed. We went all the way through December and into January without a win. I was beginning to wonder if we would win a game all season. On January 3, we played Valparaiso and lost again, by one point (73 to 72), to drop our record to 0 and 9. Worse yet, we began our winter break after that, having to go 12 days to think about that loss before we played another game. It was an amazing lesson for a first-time head coach. To this day, I wonder how we even survived.

On January 15, we played Drexel and finally won our first game, 56 to 50. It had been so humbling to go through that nine-game losing streak that I honestly don't remember feeling emotional in any way when we finally won. By that time, I had accepted the fact that we were going to lose games, which again reinforced the attitude that I was going to concentrate more on what we did as a team during practice than worry about the scoreboard results of each game.

One of the lessons that I realized I'd learned only in retrospect was how lucky I was to have experienced that rocky beginning and season at a mid-major program such as Maine's. Women's basketball was popular at the school and in the state, but our fans had realistic expectations. They knew not to expect miracles in the first year of our program. They were willing to give us the benefit of the doubt and allow us some time and space to grow as a program.

LEARNING FROM FAILURE

I feel very sorry for a lot of coaches I see now who go from being top assistants at a major program to becoming a first-time head coach at a major Division I school. The pressures and expectations are so much greater at that level that you really don't have time for failure. Everybody expects immediate success, and all of your mistakes and growing pains play out before a much larger fan base and media audience. My mistakes, and our learning curve as a program, were not nearly as scrutinized in the public eye as they would have been at a larger university. Though I was watched very closely in Maine, because basketball is very important in the state, I was able to escape the national pressure while I was there—at least initially.

I have always welcomed challenges and have rarely felt intimidated by them, and trying to work through all of those first-year mistakes was definitely educational for me. Bosses who take over a new company or organization and immediately believe they have all the answers are kidding themselves. There were things I had to learn, and the only way to do so was to endure the process.

At one point during that losing streak, I got on the phone with Joe Ciampi back at Auburn. I don't know if I was looking for a shoulder to cry on or some brotherly advice, but he immediately put me in my place, which I guess ultimately is what I should have expected. He told me, "I don't know why you are calling me," even though he did. He knew I wanted guidance; so he told me to "stay the course" and "coach for today." These simple words were so absolutely true . . . and much appreciated at that time.

Teaching the kids to get over the speed bumps of the season was not only a learning experience for them, it was for me as well. I have always been good at accepting the blame when something goes wrong. As the head coach, I knew that our team's performance was my responsibility and I was ready to take it on.

Even when I think I have done something well that doesn't quite work out the way I had hoped or expected, I tend to be really hard on myself. If I can't seem to develop a good relationship with someone, I usually assume that it must be because of something I did. This is therefore a quality I seek in leaders and mentors, because I think people tend to respect that self-deprecating quality in a person. Accepting responsibility and blame, as a leader, is necessary in becoming effective in that role. This is a part of my work ethic, my family's military background growing up, and my competitive spirit. You cannot take charge without taking in all things. There has to be singular accountability, and you hope your team and staff follow.

We ended that season with a 9 and 20 record; when it was all over, I felt a moment of poignancy that I had completed my first season as a head coach. I was teary-eyed at the team banquet, especially in thanking John for his support. He was a rock that entire year and was never swayed by any outcome. He always thought we were doing great, even when we really weren't.

Our most important victory actually came after the season, when I put together a proposal to Nike. In it, I informed the company of exactly why they should sign the Maine women's basketball team to a shoe contract. Was I naive to think they would say yes? Probably. We had won nine games and had virtually no identity and presence outside of our state boundaries. But was I going to work my tail off to try to get them to say yes? Absolutely. Nike just had to believe in our vision.

I wrote the proposal myself and included information like projected attendance and other revenue, and put a lot of time, thought, and effort into it. One of the reasons I felt so strongly about acquiring

Nike's endorsement was because there was a high school player in the state named Cindy Blodgett who wore black Nikes, and I knew recruiting her would be a tremendous boost to our program. How could I even get her to come to Maine if we did not have a deal with Nike? I doubt Cindy has any idea how much work and effort I put into the proposal. I typed it myself, which ensured slower progress, but eventually it was finished and sent out to Ed Jenka at Nike with great hope and anticipation. After that, there was nothing to do but wait for a response.

And wait I did, for three months, before I finally received the phone call from Ed that Nike was indeed going to take us on. I was never so grateful to receive 24 pairs of black sneakers in my life. This incident launched a great relationship with Nike that has continued to this day, and I've been with Nike ever since. I have given lectures for the company annually for almost 20 years. There are incredible people at Nike who have taken us on some wonderful trips. It is truly like we are a family—one that's a wonderful source of support and care. All of the coaches affiliated with Nike are very fortunate to have long-term relationships with the company. We're also afforded the opportunity to get together annually on both the women's and men's side to collaborate and share stories.

I don't think many head coaches today have experienced this kind of "need Nike shoes" pressure, since schools likely already had a shoe or equipment deal in place when most of them were hired. Despite the work I had to do and the waiting game I was forced to endure, this was one more learning experience for me, and I was extremely grateful for the way it turned out.

However, during my second year as the head coach, another learning experience produced a much different response.

The schedule for our first year had been set before the change in coaches, so I had nothing to do with who we played in the nonconference games that season. Making the schedule for the following year was, of course, my responsibility, so I assigned the task to one of my assistants.

There were not as many checks and balances in place as there are today to avoid scheduling mistakes, especially at the mid-major level. We made a major error, though, by playing one too many nonconference games.

When we discovered the mistake, it didn't seem to me to be that big a deal; I figured we would just drop a game and move on. This was simply my "reason over emotion" approach; however, reason could not trump politics this time.

Maine was in the North Atlantic Conference, along with schools such as Vermont, Boston University, New Hampshire, and Hartford—good schools, but not exactly powerhouses in women's basketball. By the time we found out about the scheduling mistake, it was too late to drop a nonconference game, so we just thought we would drop a conference game—except that nobody in the conference would agree to drop a game. Not one coach or administrator would step forward and lead to allow the top team in the league to play in the conference tournament.

This was my first real lesson in politics at the collegiate sports level. I realized nobody wanted to see Maine do well, and we were having a *much* better season in year two. We won 20 games as well as the regular season conference title, and were averaging about 3,000 fans a game.

However the conference officials decided that our error would forbid us from playing in the postseason tournament. We were the number one seed, the regular season champion, and they were going to keep us from playing because of that one meaningless extra game.

I was livid, and mad at the lack of leadership at the conference level, at Maine and at the other conference schools. The worst part of the situation was that we learned later the coach at Boston University knew very early on about our mistake; if we had known about it then, we would have had time to do something to correct the situation. Instead, Boston kept quiet until it was too late, and the conference's only recourse was to bar us from playing in the postseason tournament.

Wonderful sportsmanship and dubious character—there were life lessons for a special team in the midst of one of the greatest turnaround stories ever. How could they ever understand? Though I knew I had let them down as a leader, I felt that the pure lack of humanity and dignity of the situation was simply appalling.

What I found incredibly interesting was the reaction of the people around our program. Some were very supportive, yet others turned on us in ways I never would have imagined. I got an absolutely evil letter from a kid I had previously thought was so great telling me how

I had ruined her career. She wanted to know how I could possibly have screwed up the schedule like that. It was a horrific learning experience, one that seemed almost beyond my comprehension.

I quickly realized as this was going on that as the head coach, I had to accept the full blame and responsibility for the error. I could have passed the buck, but that would have been wrong. This scheduling error was a wonderful example of innocence, since it was a purely honest mistake. I accepted complete responsibility for the incident during the news conference that covered it. It never even crossed my mind to blame anybody else.

I knew that some of our players, their parents, and others surrounding the program were pushing me a little harder because of my age and lack of experience. They were testing me to see how hard and far they could push, to see how I would react. I won't go so far as to say they were trying to take advantage of me, but I do think they were treating me differently because I was a woman, and 26, than if I had been an older man in the same circumstances.

All of those experiences helped me to learn about myself and about balance; they taught me how to carry myself and accept my responsibilities. Some people held my age against me, but I never really saw it as an obstacle. I knew that I was enduring a baptism by fire and that the little things mattered. I also knew the reason that Maine had hired me as the head coach at the age of 26 was because I was from Maine, I had Final Four experience, and I had my MBA, which made school officials feel better about my age. My degree was almost a kind of proof that I had some level of maturity. The fact that I had pursued and secured my MBA separated me from the people against whom I competed during the hiring process.

Of course, I can't really blame these individuals for being a bit worried. Young people do have a tendency to take on more than others think they can handle without becoming all that worried about it—simply because they don't know any better. They don't even think about being afraid, or bother to listen to people who tell them that they're too young or inexperienced for the job. They really don't have any preconceived notions—just a willingness to move forward. In this way, youth is so refreshing. Combining such energy with wisdom and guidance is a dangerous combination.

I was never scared of the press, and I always tried to be respectful toward them. When we were barred from the tournament, I spoke about how the situation taught kids the wrong lesson and how we were essentially being punished for making an innocent mistake. I think a lot of people in the public eye are afraid to say what they really think today (especially to the press) because of the question of political correctness. But as far as I'm concerned, sharing appropriate truth, debate, and thoughtfulness is the only way to keep it real and interesting so that stories can be told accurately and with inspiration.

I wasn't really worried about what the press would think of me or how I would sound. I think what I said made sense to the people of Maine and earned me their support. I had stood up for my team, my players—and received a lot of flak from a lot of people for doing it. And while I still believe it was absolutely 100 percent the right thing to do, it was still a very lonely time for me. I kept questioning my judgment and asking myself over and over again, *how* I could have made such a mistake?

The most salient lesson I learned in those early years at Maine was one of humility, as well as the fact that we often encounter events that we simply cannot control. I honestly believe that these situations— and the way people react to and deal with them—truly reveal a person's genuine character. I never blamed anybody else, and I accepted total responsibility; I did what any leader should do. I had made such a public issue of the way I felt after we were barred from the tournament that I received media attention all across Maine, which resulted in my becoming an even more widely known figure. Luckily, most people in the state agreed with me, and my character, reputation, and integrity never became an issue. Instead, it solidified my position as a valued coach and leader with most Mainers.

Missing that tournament was the lowest point in my (at that time, short) career. My team lost an opportunity to compete, and I knew exactly why: The other teams were afraid of us. As the number one seed, we were favored to win the tournament; the other schools saw our mistake as a way to beat us without having to face us on the court. Telling the team I had let them down—seeing their tears and feeling their pain—was the hardest part. However, I left the locker room that day more determined and resolved to succeed than at any other point in my life.

The situation wasn't fair and it wasn't right, but it certainly was a powerful motivator for us all. We were determined to take back the lost opportunity and compete anytime, anyplace, anywhere . . . under any conditions. We were just getting started.

SEEK OUT THE WISDOM OF OTHERS

After everything that had happened during my first two years as a coach, there was one clear truth that I had wholeheartedly come to believe: I really liked my position as a head coach and enjoyed being in the business of developing people. Seeing our team's and our players' growth is something that continues to inspire me on a daily basis. I liked being in charge, shaping our plans, philosophy, and policies, and not having to answer to too many people about what we were doing. There is a true entrepreneurial spirit about becoming a coach; while there is little job security, you have great freedom to create.

One of the smartest things I did—and one of the smartest things I think anybody who is trying to learn more about his or her job should do—was to seek out older people who could help me. And I did not limit my search to my small world of basketball; I looked to both the larger university community and the entire state of Maine.

I wanted guidance from older folks, people who had been through the wars, so to speak, and who could give me advice and suggestions, but not tell me what to do. I sought their help because I wanted them to fill me in on the many facts of life I had yet to learn. As something that has really helped me during every stage of my career, this is advice I would share with anybody in *any* walk of life: There is no substitute for experience, and no substitute for building a network of friends who truly understand a coach's (or any profession, for that matter) life and perspective.

I am stunned nowadays by the lack of young coaches who actively seek mentors. The ability to see what has come before and learn from others has always been very important to me, and it is crucial for anyone who will likely endure the same events and circumstances. No one is an instant coach—or an instant anything. You are a product of the small, seemingly irrelevant but truly monumental choices you make every single day. Coaching, like so many other callings, is a delicate craft that must be nurtured by many, and the person developing his or her career must be the one to initiate, listen, and learn.

I found out early on in this profession that there are a lot of pseudo-coaches; in other words, they act the part, but don't really coach. They develop cozy relationships with a few select individuals instead of having the courage to learn how to coach everyone. Good coaches have to be willing to learn—and to be wrong. That's the only way to be successful; and that's something I realized from the beginning of my career. Too many people think (incorrectly, of course) that coaching is something anybody can do, that just because people have played or gathered general knowledge of a sport, they are qualified to coach. Coaching is a *learned* craft; being fans or playing the game does not make someone a coach. There are very few individuals who form the elite level of coaches, and those are the people from whom I have tried to learn as much as possible.

I wanted to know if I was doing something inappropriate, to learn the proper ways of operating at the university level. People such as George Jacobson, our faculty representative, and Anne Pooler, who is now the dean of the College of Education and Human Development at Maine, were very kind and gracious with their time and suggestions for me.

I was never shy about asking for guidance. Having an inner circle of older friends you can talk to is important for anybody in business, but especially for younger people just starting out in a given field or industry. My willingness to ask others for help falls completely in line with my personality as a young girl who was never afraid to try something new or to be wrong. I was never shy about asking people what they thought about a particular topic or issue.

I knew I did not have all of the answers; but I also knew that I wanted to get them, and wasn't afraid to keep asking questions until I did.

I had also been able to bring in some of my own recruits by the third year at Maine, including perhaps the best-ever player to come out of the state—Cindy Blodgett. I had been working like crazy to get Cindy on board almost since the day I walked into the office. As I mentioned before, one of the reasons I had worked so hard on acquiring our Nike deal was to make certain Cindy came to Maine.

Cindy captured the attention of everyone in the state when she was in high school, in a way I have never seen a high school player, male or female, do before or since. She lived 50 minutes south of the Maine campus, and every school in the country was recruiting her. Cindy won four state championships at Lawrence High School and was the Gatorade player of the year in the state as a sophomore, junior, and senior. She is the all-time leading scorer in Maine high school history with 2,596 career points. She was a complete phenom. Her final choices came down to Maine, Notre Dame, and Colorado; I was absolutely thrilled when we discovered she had chosen to come to Maine. All of my staff members had done an exceptional recruiting job; doing so had been a true labor of love, and both Cindy and I worked to get to know each other better throughout the recruiting process.

One of the fans Cindy had attracted in high school was writer Tabitha King, wife of author Stephen King, both of whom are from Maine. Tabitha took such an interest in Cindy that she wrote a book about her while she was still in high school. Cindy's plans to come to school in Maine piqued the Kings' interest in our team and gave me a chance to develop a very nice relationship with them. Tabitha and Stephen actually met in the University of Maine library, and their beautiful estate was kitty-corner from the tiny apartment where John and I lived when we first came to Maine.

I met Tabitha before I met Stephen, whom I met when he brought their son Owen to a Maine function I happened to be attending. Even though I had not read all of his books, I of course knew who he was. I introduced myself but started talking to Owen, who was playing basketball at his school, almost immediately. I think Stephen was struck with the fact that I wasn't taken in by his fame and persona, but instead was interested in his son's activities, and we hit it off. My energy is always drawn to kids, because there are no filters with young people—just a straightforward, welcoming openness that makes talking to them thoroughly enjoyable.

Stephen and Tabitha started coming to our games, and having Cindy there prompted them to become very enthusiastic, supportive fans. I liked both of them very much, and tried to respect their privacy and fame. Still, they were the kind of people who would do anything to help out our program. I happened to mention one time that I wished we could change our wooden backboards in the practice gym to fiberglass but that we didn't have the money in the budget to do it. Not long after that conversation, I walked into the gym and noticed we had new fiberglass backboards. Stephen and Tabitha had paid the bill . . . but never said a word about it.

Stephen was a big fan of Maine and of Mainers, and especially of people who stayed in Maine. I think that was why they took such an interest in Cindy—along with the fact that she was such a gifted player, of course. The Kings began to actively support women's athletics; one of the most thrilling experiences of my life was when they invited me to go with them on their Learjet to New York to attend a dinner supporting the Women's Sports Foundation. They had paid a lot of money to buy a table, and I was honored to be their guest.

John and I were adjusting well to Maine. Even though he had not received a full-time position at the University, he was teaching in the economics department, and he had fallen in love with all the state has to offer. Despite the setback we experienced in being banned from the postseason conference tournament, the 20-win season in my second year as coach energized me and got me incredibly excited about the future.

John and I also soon had another reason to be thankful, when our daughter, Maddie, was born on August 31, 1994. One topic I could talk endlessly and candidly about with women is that of the mistakes I made when handling Maddie's birth and the process of becoming a new parent.

Since Maddie's due date was September 18, I thought that, at the end of August, we were still a couple of weeks away from her birth. However, at about 5:30 in the morning on August 31, 1994, I went to the restroom and realized that my water had broken. I went back to bed, and started getting extremely sharp pains about 45 minutes later. I told John about them, and his immediate reaction was "It can't be the baby." The instructors in the Lamaze classes we had taken prepared us for the fact that the birth process is going to be long. So when I told John I thought I was in labor, he didn't believe it; yet I was in such profound pain by 6:30 that I could barely speak.

At 6:45 AM I was on the telephone with the doctor, who told me to get to the hospital immediately. I was very, very scared when we finally reached the hospital about 7:15 AM. I could not speak to anybody, and was in so much pain that I thought something *had* to be wrong. I couldn't walk, which John couldn't believe. I was having trouble convincing the people in the hospital that everything was happening way too fast. Finally a nurse took me into a room to examine me, and the look on her face was priceless as she instructed me not to move or to push. I knew at that moment that the baby was coming—*soon*. I felt so powerful and so vindicated that I was *not* being a hypochondriac and that I was justified in my feeling that everything was happening so quickly.

I felt so relieved that nothing was wrong; I was just having a baby! At five minutes to eight, John walked into the room, ready to settle in for the long day. When the doctor told him the baby was about to come, his face expressed a look of complete shock. Maddie was born at 8:04 AM—a completely healthy baby girl.

Because I was young and naive, and still had the attitude that I could do it all, the biggest mistake I made was failing to take enough time to recover from the pregnancy and birth before getting back to work. I spent one night in the hospital and then was back working full-time (albeit from home) the next day.

It took a couple of years to catch up with me, but when it did, I found myself back in the hospital.

I really did think that I could somehow take care of every area of my life—my job, my child, my marriage—without taking proper care of myself. I was not trying to shortchange either my baby or my work; I just honestly thought I would not have to make sacrifices in either area. This Superwoman mentality came from being a Title IX baby, as well as having support all my life as an athlete. I didn't think that being a mom would be any different from the other roles I'd played or responsibilities I'd had, and I didn't see any reason to change my schedule or work habits. I had been fortunate to coach for two years without having a child to look after, and I realize looking back now how easy it had been to coach without having the added responsibility of being a parent.

All young working mothers face the challenges of trying to balance their jobs and motherhood, and, if they are like me, they don't think anything can stop them. I was a classic example of this kind of multi-tasking, using a breast pump double-fisted and watching game film at the same time when I came home for lunch. I learned in short order that I had a responsibility to both my job *and* my child, and the two didn't always coexist easily. I am so glad I had both of my children when I was coaching at Maine, because even though it was an intense job, I didn't experience anything close to the pressures that exist at larger schools like Michigan State or Duke. I don't know how any woman could be coaching at a school of that caliber and give birth to a child without it affecting her health, sanity, job performance, and overall happiness.

I know some women who claim that they're going to have a baby at some point; my honest advice to them is to plan ahead if you can. While it was not my plan to have my kids when I was coaching at a mid-major school, I am certainly glad it happened then. John played a huge role in taking care of Maddie as we got set to start the 1994–1995 season. I am fortunate to have a real man in John—one who can do anything and everything. He basically raised Maddie from the time she was a baby.

It is hard to know how your partner will respond when you begin a new chapter of your lives together. The lesson this experience taught me is how important it is to choose the right partner for your life. None of this would have been possible without John, whose easygoing manner and love for family was clearly evident. I was always stunned at his natural ability to care for our kids when they were babies. The "do it all" reality affects so many parents, single or not. Finding critical quiet moments within the high-paced day is so important. "Me" time is a real need and must be carved out for each day. Walking the dog, early morning exercise, or even an unrushed morning can go a long way to reenergizing. Planning is so important.

Our biggest nonconference game that season took place against Alabama on January 5. It was a big deal because they were ranked tenth in the country, coming off an appearance in the Final Four, and we had gotten them to come to our place. Mid-majors in the 1990s had the same problem as mid-majors do today when it comes to scheduling: Most of the power schools will agree to play you, but only on their turf. And no big school team wants to play a mid-major if they think there's a chance they might lose. Alabama had a 10 and 1 record and was averaging 94 points a game, and nobody was predicting that we could pull off the upset, but, as the cliché goes, that's why you play the game. I told our team at practice that they might as well not show up if they didn't think they could win . . . but they might miss a heck of an opportunity.

I was an emotional wreck before the game, and it had nothing to do with worrying about Alabama. A dear friend, Walter Hunt, who ran Dead River Oil Company in Bangor, died of a heart attack while playing basketball. He was only in his fifties, and it was a terrible shock. He had been a real mentor to me; he and his wife often played golf with John and me, and I adored him. The wake was the same night as our face-off against Alabama, so I got dressed and went there before going to the game.

Walter's death was so unexpected, and everybody at the wake was crying, including myself. It was very draining. I stayed as long as I could before I had to leave, and the last thing in the world I felt like doing at that moment was coaching a game. All the fans were pouring into Alfond Arena as I arrived, and though I tried to dry my tears, I just didn't feel that I could turn off my emotions that quickly.

One of my assistant coaches, Lamar Boutwell, saw how torn up I was and pulled me out into the hallway.

"Are you all right?" he asked.

"I can't do this; I can't coach this game," I told him. I started talking about the wake and about Walter, and Lamar was right next to me with a very stern look in his eyes and said calmly, "But you will."

Then he said, in a very firm voice, "These girls need you." It surprised me, because I didn't know Lamar had that in him. He was a happy-go-lucky guy, but he really took a serious tone that day. He said it and walked away, and I was stunned and proud that he had taken on such a role.

Lamar's words had snapped me back to attention. The game started, and before any of the record-setting 5,000 fans had sat down, we were behind 8 to 0.

I called a time-out and ripped into the team. We woke up, Cindy scored 30 points in her tenth college game, and we hung on to win

75 to 73, as Alabama missed a three-pointer at the buzzer. To this day, I think it is the most exciting single game—men's or women's—ever played in Alfond Arena.

The victory immediately energized our program and gave us national credibility. The media asked me immediately after the game (and for the next couple of days) what the win meant. I kept saying that it was a good starting point, and I honestly meant that. No matter how big it was, a single victory in the regular season would not take us to where we wanted to go, and that was the NCAA Tournament.

"The best thing for us to have is a total challenge," I said to the media. "If you don't taste what's at the top, you're never going to get there. If we fall on our face, we pick ourselves up and learn. If we're successful, we drive it home. But you've got to take the chance. You've got to go for it."

I was always trying to inspire my players in every way that I could. I told them we were going to go to the Final Four. I was honestly convinced that we could develop the program to where it would be at that level. I also did not have to remind the players of how our fellow conference members had treated us the previous year, knowing the only way they could beat us in the conference tournament was to keep us from playing because of the scheduling mix-up.

Thus motivated, we roared through the league schedule with a 14 and 2 record—then won the postseason tournament. We had won 21 of our last 23 games, which included 13 in a row; our last win, over Northeastern, also brought with it a spot in the NCAA Tournament—a first in the history of our program.

The happy feelings lasted less than 24 hours, because, despite all of the hard work we'd done and accomplishments we'd achieved, the NCAA selection committee gave us a number 16—that is the last seed in the East regional. Our first-round opponent was number one ranked Connecticut, who we would have to play on UConn's home court.

Our players gasped and groaned as the team watched the selection show on television. We had just received yet another lesson about life and politics in women's basketball. A sixteenth seed was too low for our work and accomplishments; however, it was a reality of regional scheduling and being a newcomer to the NCAA Tournament as well. There is, of course, no way to know what would have happened had we received a better draw; but we didn't have a say in the matter. I kept telling myself and the team *not* to concentrate on the outcome of that final game, but to think instead about everything that we had accomplished in that season—how far we had come, even if the year did end with a big disappointment.

The most immediate and final result is always the one that sticks with you, and basketball players (and coaches) are not immune to that feeling. Yet in both basketball and in life, it is important to keep everything in balance and perspective. It had been a great year, and I honestly believed that even better days were to come.

Coach P instructing her team during a game at the University of Virginia on February 24, 2011.
Source: Jason Kruse

CHAPTER 7 QUESTIONS

• Do you have mentors in your life? What makes them suitable as mentors?

• There are people who are detractors at all times in life. Can you handle those who choose not to support you? What do you do to not allow these people to affect your success?

• Can you cultivate older mentors in your life from whose experience you can benefit?

• Do you have a strong life balance between your work and your family?

• Have you been challenged by an ultimate opponent in your life, currently or in the past? How do you respond?

NOT ALL OF YOUR PLAYERS (OR EMPLOYEES) WILL GET ALONG WITH EACH OTHER

THE OTHER SIDE OF SUCCESS

One reality of coaching that also applies to the business world is that even a little bit of success gets others to notice you and pay attention.

It happens every year: A coach takes a team on an unexpected run through the NCAA Tournament, whether on the men's or women's side, and suddenly, he or she is a hot name and is linked to every job opening available. Even though I knew this happened, it was not something with which I was entirely familiar or something I expected to happen to me. That was, until I got back home to Maine and my telephone rang.

Long Beach State University in California was looking for a new coach for their women's team and wondered if I would be interested in talking to them. Sure, why not? Because I'm a Navy brat who enjoys traveling, seeing the world, and gathering information directly, it made sense to me to explore this opportunity.

I don't know if I would have put down odds on the chance that I would accept a job offer had one been made, but I didn't really see any harm in going out there and investigating the situation. Long Beach's athletic director, Dave O'Brien, was a terrific person and talented at his job. His vision and support made an immediate impact on me.

One of the realities of coaching at Maine (which, again, is the situation at almost every mid-major) is that coaches always find themselves in some kind of budget crunch. There is never enough money to run your program the way you think it should be run—to pay your assistants a good salary, to travel the way you think you should, to have the training facilities and support staff around that a team really needs to be successful. So I think my intention in talking to Long Beach State was to educate myself on how they ran their program and to see whether I could bring about some changes to our program after engaging with them personally.

When the news got out that I was going to California to interview for the job, however, it was as though I already had announced I was leaving. How could I do this? I was a Maine kid. Didn't I care about my state? Many people, including members of the media, said and wrote some pretty harsh things, which really surprised me at the time.

What bothered me the most was that for one of the first times since I had begun coaching, I thought the criticism was being directed at the fact I was a woman in my field. Something about the treatment I was experiencing told me that it might be indicative of gender bias. People said I was "leveraging" the Maine job against the job at Long Beach State. Yet when a male coach goes to interview about a possible new job, he is simply "exploring the market." The media called my actions shameful, unwarranted, unfair, and self-driven.

This was the most ridiculous and uneducated example of journalism I thought I would ever see. I had to make a decision about whether to fight to improve the situation at Maine or to try to move on. Going on the Long Beach interview was my way of fighting for my team—learning more and gaining information. I was proud of my investigative nature and my honesty with all parties involved.

I had to be an advocate for our team the only way I knew how. If the school administrators really thought there was a chance I might leave (and wanted to keep me there), it stood to reason they would try to figure out a way to budget more money for our team. There was never an issue with my salary; it was about getting everything we needed to be a top-flight program, one that could compete on a yearly basis with the best teams in the country. This was especially important given our most recent experience in the NCAA Tournament. We knew we had a long way to go.

The situation with the women's team was widely discussed and really ruffled some traditional feathers at Maine. There were a lot of people who were happy that we had done well; however, they thought we had reached a high enough level and didn't see why we couldn't just be satisfied with where we were. Many people feel satisfaction and a sense of relief after some initial success. Yet this is what drives me the most to improve. Failing to do so might cause you to overlook some important successful developments as you keep your eye on the ultimate prize. It is critical to enjoy the ride along the way (something with which I still struggle to this day), but commitment to process is what endures.

I could never understand the logic of being happy where you are. It would be akin to a company reaching a certain sales figure for the year and letting all of the salespeople know that this was good enough, that they shouldn't bother trying to improve the following year. This approach simply baffled me. I was looking for growth in every area of women's basketball at Maine, while some people were okay with the status quo. I was talking about going to the Final Four and trying to win a National Championship. Why didn't other people have the same goals and vision that I had? Did they really believe in all that we were trying to do?

Luckily, there were some special people at Maine who *did* agree with me. In turning down the chance to move to Long Beach State, I was able to secure some additional funding for our program. This, in turn, put us on almost the same level as the men's team, and gave me a new sense of enthusiasm to make our team as good as it could be. I wanted to prove the previous year's success was not just a one-time occurrence, but also truly an exciting beginning to a new era of women's basketball at Maine.

I was always grateful that there never seemed to be a problem of resentment from the men's team. Coaching at Maine gave me the chance to build quality relationships with the men's team's coaches, an attribute that would prove valuable to me in later years. Maine's men's basketball coach through the 1996 season was Rudy Keeling, someone with whom I got along very well, and even danced with on the court one time at Midnight Madness. John Giannini became the coach when he left, and we worked well together, too, sharing stories and frustrations. When both men's and women's programs work well together, the entire athletic department and university benefit.

Before the season began, however, I received a personal wake-up call. In late October 1995, shortly after practices had begun, I found myself in the hospital and then at home in bed, under doctor's orders to rest.

In addition to the stress of interviewing with Long Beach State and trying to get the upgrades for our team at Maine, my summer had included travel to a tournament in Belgium, recruiting trips, and trying to take care of Maddie, who had just turned one. I didn't manage myself and my needs very well, and became very, very tired as a result. I had always insisted that I was fine and that I could do everything, including coming home at noon to feed Maddie at the same time I was watching film and taking notes. When Maddie switched to solid food, however, and I had the added stress of planning meals, going to the store, and so forth, I hit a breaking point. Up to that point, I had learned how to balance my life and really be a Superwoman and do it all. Maddie, however, dared to outgrow infancy on me; her transition from baby to toddler really left me with a feeling of inadequacy that I had never felt before.

Since I had never learned to cook, Maddie's food had been provided for her in a little bottle or in those handy little jars of fruits and vegetables up to this point in her life. Now it was up to me to make certain she was getting the right food to eat. Thinking about her food and her diet was, oddly, a difficult adjustment to make, and I wondered if other women had that problem. I thought to myself, "You've got to be kidding me. What am I going to do about feeding this kid?" It really was a big fear for me. I needed to be in the gym, working, not trying to figure out what to give my child for dinner. While John was certainly reassuring, the fear and concern seemed to be a culmination of colliding responsibilities as I rode the wave of the so-called Superwoman balance.

Somehow the awesome responsibility of mothering manifested itself as Maddie went from being bottle fed to solid food, then from jar food to the real thing. This transition utterly depleted my energy and made me vulnerable to fatigue. It was the first time as a mother (and as a coach) that I ever experienced something like that. I started seeing everything from the lens of a mom, and felt as though I wasn't being a good one if I didn't come home every night and make dinner.

LEARNING BALANCE, RESTORING ENERGY

Youth and experience can occasionally cause people to make silly decisions, and that is what happened to me. In trying to prove that I could handle everything, I was handling nothing. My body was stuck on Belgium time; I was tired and not sleeping well. I had to learn what I needed to do to take care of myself. I always prided myself on being able to restore energy in my life—and, for the first time, it was just was not happening.

I knew that my inability to do so was a sign that I was trying to juggle too many things and that I needed to make some changes in my lifestyle. The demands in all areas of my life were colliding simultaneously. I really had no intention of slowing down; however, I did know that I had to make some changes in my schedule (such as limiting speaking and social engagements) that would allow me to have a bit more downtime during which I could restore my energy. I had been traveling all over the state for appearances, and I wasn't turning down any offers. I knew that had to change. It was time for me to grow up a bit in every aspect of my life.

My biggest priority, other than to my family, was still to my team, and I was happy to see that our players had come back excited and motivated to be even better than we were in the 1994–1995 season.

It turned out to be a very special year. We went through the conference season undefeated and had a school-record 19-game winning streak. Cindy Blodgett led the nation in scoring, averaging almost 28 points a game; we won the postseason tournament and earned our second trip in a row to the NCAA Tournament. The selection committee was a little more generous this time, seeding us eleventh and sending us to Charlottesville, Virginia, for a first-round game against sixth-seeded George Washington.

We jumped out to a 9 to 0 lead and remained ahead four minutes into the second half. It was all downhill from there, however, and the end result was our second first-round loss.

The worst thing about losing in the NCAA Tournament is that it brings such a dramatic and crushing end to a team's season. The girls' disappointment was obvious as we prepared to leave Virginia to fly back to Maine the next morning. This was a game we thought we could win, and we lost. We had not lost a game since the end of December and had really enjoyed the winning streak.

Yet I was not going to let that loss affect how proud I was of all of the good things our team had accomplished. I know it sounded like a broken record, because I had said much the same thing the previous year, but it was true. We didn't win an NCAA game, but we got better as a team. We improved, which is any coach's goal in *any* year. Viewing success or failure merely in terms of winning a national title would result in a heck of a lot of disappointed coaches every year.

EXPECTATIONS FOR THE FUTURE

Looking back at my first four years at Maine, I was very proud of what we had accomplished and excited about the future. We had built a solid base of enthusiastic and supportive fans, ranking 19th in the country and outdrawing the men's team. We had powerful support from Maine Senators Collins and Snowe, as well as Governor Angus King. We had earned respect and recognition on the national stage. We had made Maine residents believe they could compete with anybody in the country—a special vision that the team provided.

Though I was pleased with our overall performance and situation, I was not satisfied. I wanted more. Pursuing the ultimate level was always my personal goal, and one I wanted for our players as well.

The job that was open and attractive after that season was at Florida State. Though I agreed to listen to what they had to say, I quickly took my name out of consideration. Yet I was happy this time that members of the media weren't labeling me as a villain for simply looking into a job at another school. I loved the fact that reporters seemed to be more positive and forward thinking in this instance. I also believed that the way in which I had "handled the market" during the prior incident had, even in just a small way, brought more equity in perception relative to male and female coaches. As Pete Warner of the *Bangor Daily News* wrote, "Regardless of the job you perform, you must always leave the door slightly ajar for promising opportunities. . . . Smart, successful people are always going to be in demand."

My approach with Florida State was akin to my intention in meeting with Long Beach State: I wanted to use the attention and interest from another school to help our program. I really was determined to see how far we could take the Maine program, and I didn't think we had that answer yet.

Another obstacle we faced was that we lost a player I didn't expect us to lose before the start of the season. This episode made me refocus my attention on the importance of creating and maintaining chemistry among a team's players and trying to develop that team-first attitude.

We had recruited and signed Trisha Ripton before the 1993 season, one year before we signed Cindy Blodgett. Unfortunately, I didn't know until much later that Trisha and Cindy had a strained relationship because of the attention and praise Cindy had received in high school. Players who are as good as Cindy are bound to generate some jealousy from their peers. I didn't really see any problems between the two girls when they played together; however, I guess it became more of an issue than I had initially realized.

I loved having Cindy and Trisha on the floor together, and it hurt me to know that Trisha was forgoing her senior year at Maine.

When something like that happens, a coach has to analyze all of the factors involved to see whether she has made any mistakes along the way that could have led to a different outcome. As with any team sport or any business environment, it is simply a fact of life that not all of your players (or employees, for that matter) are going to get along with each other. But any kind of manager worth his or her salt must attempt to ensure that a disagreement between team members doesn't affect the group's (or the company's) overall performance. Since I hadn't seen anything like that brewing over the previous two years, the development with Trisha took me completely by surprise.

As much as I would have liked for Trisha to play that season, I had to respect her decision, and the rest of us had to move forward as a team. We did have three senior starters returning, plus Cindy, who was now a junior. However, we also had a very aggressive nonconference schedule—one that included games against six teams either ranked in the preseason poll or coming off appearances in the previous NCAA Tournament. Aggressive scheduling has been a constant theme throughout my career. I simply love the challenge a tough schedule presents; I always have and always will.

Whether those tough games were the reason or not, we were better prepared for conference play and once again rolled to the league title. We went 17 and 1 and won 18 of our next 19 games, capped by another conference tournament championship, which put us back into the NCAA Tournament for the third consecutive year. However, we still had not been able to win that first game in the tournament. This time we were seeded 13th and sent to Baton

Rouge, Louisiana, to once again play an outstanding LSU team on its home court.

Everyone was out relaxing by the pool at our hotel after practice, including band members, cheerleaders, and a lot of donors who had made the trip from Maine to Louisiana. John and Maddie were with me, and I'd been talking to a lot of people before we left to head back to our room. John was in the lead, and Maddie (who was four at this time) was behind him and in front of me. Someone came up to me from behind and grabbed my shoulder, and when I turned around to see who it was, I lost sight of Maddie. After talking to the individual, I turned back around and didn't see either John or Maddie, so I naturally assumed that Maddie had followed John into our hotel room.

Before I could go into the room, more people came up and wanted a minute of my time. I ended up walking with them back toward the pool, when I suddenly had a very sick feeling in my stomach that I know was a mother's intuition. I just had a great feeling of fear that something was wrong, but I didn't know what it was. I started to pick up all of my things and head back to our room.

What I didn't know was that when I had lost sight of Maddie, she had not walked into our hotel room but had instead had kept going. She had actually walked across the side street into a parking lot and then to a gas station, which was right next to a highway. Before I could get back to our room, a woman came screaming out toward the pool. She was holding Maddie. I looked at her in complete shock as she yelled in her Southern accent, "*Whose baby is this?*" I felt like the worst, most inadequate mother in the world. How could I be so absolutely irresponsible? I was stunned and shocked, and immediately ran to get her.

The fact I could have lost my child because I was tending to a supporter trying to get my attention evoked a sense of guilt that ran from my head to my toes. I was completely shaken by that experience. I took Maddie and went back to our room. And the strange thing was that even though I was scared out of my mind, Maddie wasn't crying, which almost made it worse. My child didn't need to be comforted, but *I* did.

That experience really brought on a seesaw of emotions for me. One minute I felt like the most incompetent mother on the planet, and the next, I was guiding my powerful team in front of 6,000 hostile LSU fans. I had to calm down from the shock of losing Maddie and get our team ready to play LSU. Luckily, the years I had spent at Auburn made me very familiar with LSU as well as their coach, Sue Gunter, whom I loved and respected. I really felt it was a major disadvantage for us to have to play so far away from home, at a site that was very inconvenient for all of our fans. But I also knew that it was a part of growing a consistent NCAA Tournament program.

I knew it had been another good year even after we lost and headed back home; however, I was once again disappointed that it had ended this way. The media was starting to question whether we were good enough to win a game in the tournament, and I was wondering if we needed that elusive victory to prove that we really had gotten better as a team and were continuing to do so.

I remember asking myself a lot of questions at that time: Was I wrong when I kept talking about how good we could be and how we were improving? Was it unrealistic to think that Maine could win an NCAA Tournament game? Could I have the success that I really wanted to have as a coach at Maine, or should I pay more attention to schools that I knew would, in all likelihood, offer me a job once again?

These were all tough questions, and I didn't know if I had all of the answers. As I thought about it, however, I became increasingly determined to try to prove that we could, indeed, win at Maine. Cindy was going to be a senior the next season. We had a solid group of young players returning and had signed some terrific recruits as well.

I didn't want to have to deal with rumors and questions about whether I was going anywhere. Therefore, I made it known almost as soon as the season ended that I was not interested in pursuing any other job offers and would be staying at Maine.

It was hard to believe that Cindy was going to be a senior and that I would have only one more season to coach her. She had accomplished a great deal in her first three years, and I knew her endeavors were going to impact our program long after she was gone. Having Cindy on our team helped us raise our standards and made us strive for higher goals—namely, winning championships. I still think we faced an inferiority complex in many ways, an attitude that Mainers just seemed to be born with. But Cindy was doing her best to destroy the myth that we were destined to be the underdog. There didn't seem to be anything that she couldn't do.

Of course, there's no way that a one player can produce a championship single-handedly, no matter how gifted and talented he or she is. But I really thought that *this* season, we had enough quality players surrounding Cindy to allow us to break through and finally win that elusive NCAA Tournament game—and make a run for the championship.

The fact that I was beginning my sixth season of coaching at Maine seemed incredible to me. The time had just flown by. I wish I could have taken it more slowly and been able to take a step back and appreciate everything as it happened. Most coaches struggle to do this, especially young ones, because we are always too wrapped up in the moment, preparing for the next game, to really enjoy what is occurring. You enjoy it throughout the experience, and you reflect later.

Except for the three frustrating losses in the first round of the NCAA Tournament, the previous four years had really been amazing. We had lost a total of five conference games, going a combined total of 61 and 5 in the league during that span, and we had a lot to be happy about.

I honestly expected my team that sixth year to be the one that broke the barrier and clinched a spot in the national rankings. I truly thought we'd earn more than a number 11 seed in the tournament, thereby cementing Cindy's legacy as one of the greatest women basketball players in history on one of the greatest teams ever at Maine.

So, what happened? Well, this was yet another great learning moment in my career. I had agreed to let our team be the subject of a documentary about the season. The cameras moved in, and as much as we all tried to ignore them and go about our business, they ultimately proved to be a distraction. I am convinced we lost games because of it. This was another example of my naïveté: assuming we would still do everything exactly as we had done *without* the cameras and that we all could balance the time in and out of the spotlight effortlessly.

Whether the cameras were to blame or not, something happened to us that has happened to a lot of teams, at all levels, in all sports, throughout the years. We didn't play as well as our publicity clippings; other teams were energized to play us; and we forgot to play *our* way—connected, focused, and in the moment. We were handling others' expectations instead of just enjoying the process. Though the documentary was wonderful for women and girls in sports, it took more energy for us to do things and put more emphasis on individuals as the stories of the season unfolded. During one disastrous stretch, we lost 5 of 11 conference games—the same number we had lost out of 66 games during the previous four seasons. Instead of winning a fifth consecutive conference title, we finished second.

Luckily for us, the conference tournament was in *our* building that year, and we rose to the challenge. Cindy, who was playing for the last time in her home state, scored 22 points as we edged Vermont 81 to 80 to win the postseason tournament and the league's automatic berth in the NCAA field. It was pure poetry to see the team battle a terrific Vermont team and to see our team member Jamie Cassidy hit the winning basket.

I knew the NCAA selection committee was going to take our lack of success during the regular season into account. I was immune to the procedure by this time, and really had no reaction on learning we were a 13 seed again. We were sent to Raleigh, North Carolina, to play North Carolina State—the tenth-ranked team in the country—on their home court.

I also thought that the "desire switch" that had clicked on for the conference championship game might stay lit and give us that extra gear we had not found in the NCAA Tournament for the past three years. I knew this team was good enough to win; the question was whether they would play that way.

The game wasn't close, as North Carolina State won 89 to 64, a very disappointing end to a disappointing season. Little did I know then that Kay Yow would go on to lead NC State to a Final Four, and how much of a mentor she would become for me years later when I went to Duke, despite the fact I would get to spend just a couple of far too brief years with her. I became emotional at the postgame news conference, sitting in the interview room with Cindy and fellow senior Sandi Carver, realizing their careers had come to an end. I was so proud of them and what they had meant to our program. I just wished their final game could have had a better result.

I knew that trying to replace Cindy and Sandi would be difficult, but we had other talented players returning. Maybe this season had

been a great education for them. It would be a challenge, but I welcomed that, just like any other challenge that had come my way.

However, I didn't know at that point that the next challenge
I would face would come on a much more personal level.

**Coach P with her daughter, Maddie,
in Maine during the summer of 2010.**
Source: Personal Collection

CHAPTER 8 QUESTIONS

- Are you in a position to negotiate in your current place in your career?
  Is it healthy for your working relationship to negotiate?
- How do you obtain more resources in your job?
- Can you work with all the different departments within your organization?
- Have you ever made any parental mistakes that were humbling
  beyond measure?

9

LIFE IS MORE
than the Game

AWAY FROM THE COURT, MY PRIORITIES CHANGE

In the spring of 1998, I became pregnant again. I was excited, because John and I wanted another child. My first pregnancy with Maddie had been so easy that I thought that would be the case again. I had recorded my first hole in one on the golf course and was doing flip turns while swimming laps in the pool in the months before I had Maddie. I was a very active pregnant lady.

This time, however, I found myself at the doctor's office after only a few months when he gave me the news that I had suffered a miscarriage.

As the doctor explained to me what had happened, I was depleted of all energy. It was a devastating and brutal experience. One of the most difficult parts for me, other than the physical pain of going through the medical procedure, was that it happened on the same day that Cindy Blodgett was drafted by the WNBA. The timing was surreal. We had scheduled a news conference, and I had to be there.

I went straight from the doctor's office, where I had thought I was going for a normal checkup. I had to fight to hold myself together at the press conference, and could not say anything about what had happened to me. It was Cindy's big day; I wanted to be there for her, and was certainly happy for her. I had to hide the pain and grief that I was truly feeling. It was the best day of her life and the worst day of mine.

I was trying to dry my tears and compose myself as I drove to the news conference. It was very hard—indeed, practically impossible—to balance the two events that took place that day. It was a daunting challenge to stay composed and poised, given the personal trauma I was facing. I had no idea how I was going to hold it in, but I somehow managed to do it. As soon as the press conference ended and I was back in my car heading home, I was crying again.

I learned so much enduring this experience. Experiencing a miscarriage is as hard psychologically for women as it is physically; and, as with most difficult moments in life, there really are no instructions about what people should say to you or how they should react. I needed people to tell me they were very sorry for my loss, and to give me the time and space to mourn and deal with both the mental and physical pain. Some people tried to be nonchalant about it, making statements such as, "It's okay, you'll have another one." Though I'm sure their intentions were good, that was incredibly hard for me to hear.

I felt that I needed to speak with women who had undergone the same thing; I wanted signs of thoughtfulness, not for people to ignore what had happened. No matter what doctors tell women who endure such an experience, it is natural for a mother to feel guilty and to think that the tragedy was somehow her fault and that she could have prevented it if she had done something differently. I certainly thought this way myself.

I needed to be around people who were calm and sensitive and who could give me that space and time. My players were too young to know what to say, and my assistant coaches didn't know how to act. Everybody was scared to say or do the wrong thing, and it really was an awkward period of time.

I took a little time to evaluate my life as I recovered. I realized that I likely had been pushing myself too hard and that this was yet another wake-up call that I needed. I knew my life was forever changed because of what happened. I still vowed to be as intense a coach as I had always been, but away from the court, my priorities and perspective had vastly matured.

TEAM IN TRANSITION

Our team was transitioning at this time, too, after losing Cindy to the professional ranks. I was happy for her; she was headed to her new life in Cleveland, and I knew her success at the next level would produce only more recognition for her and support for our program.

I wasn't really worried about how we were going to replace Cindy. We had a corps of good players, and I expected us to be as competitive as we had been during the years that Cindy and our other senior, Sandi Carver, were there.

Of course, expectations are fleeting. No coach really knows what is going to happen once the ball is tossed in the air, which is what makes every sport exciting. All I wanted for our team that season, as I do in any year, was to play as well as we could play and see how far it would take us.

I think the players carried a little extra motivation with them into the season, too; they wanted to prove that we had been more than a one-person team during the previous four years. That kind of attitude can be a good and healthy thing for any group, team, or company.

We could not have played much better during the league schedule. We won 17 out of 18 games, losing only at Northeastern, and headed into the postseason conference tournament with a great deal of confidence. We advanced to the finals, but then suffered a tough 57 to 55 loss to Northeastern again.

The serious result of the loss in the tournament finals meant that we would not be awarded the league's automatic bid to the NCAA Tournament. For the first time, we were relying on the selection committee to reward our great season (23 and 6) with an at-large bid. Since it would be the first ever for a team in our conference, I was not certain it would happen. I was hopeful, but tried to remain realistic about our chances when thinking about all of the teams that wanted one of those bids.

The team really didn't know what to expect when we gathered to watch the selection show. I would not have been greatly surprised if we'd been left out entirely. As it was, we had to wait until almost the end of the show—the next to last team announced—before we found out we had made it. The feeling in the room went from low to incredibly high. Everybody was jubilant, crying, and hugging each other. The end result didn't really make much sense; not only were we picked, we received the highest seed ever in our five consecutive trips to the tournament. We were the number 10 seed and a first-round matchup against Stanford in Norfolk, Virginia.

In retrospect, I think the fact that we were selected as an at-large team instead of earning the automatic bid kind of raised our spirits a little bit. We knew we had been given a second chance. Everyone was acting silly at practice the next day, still celebrating the bid, and I had to come down hard on them. One of our players, Lacey Stone, tried to hug me, and I pushed her away and told the team, "It's time to get to work." The hugging and celebrating were over; we had work to do. Most of it involved getting in the right frame of mind after the at-large bid announcement. We so appreciated the respect that all Maine teams had contributed to this at-large berth. "Staying in the moment" is a critical component to right thinking in both the athletic and business worlds. Moving forward, turning the page to the next moment, is an invaluable component for long-term success.

I was on the hunt for any extra edge I could find before the game. I even read *Shooting from the Outside*, a book by Stanford coach Tara VanDerveer about leading the 1996 U.S. Women's basketball team to Olympic gold. It was still in my bag as I went to a news conference where Tara happened to be present; she saw it and asked if I had enjoyed it. Maybe something I learned reading the book made the difference in the game. Although there was nothing specific in the book that helped me in the game, just the experience of reading it and becoming familiar with Tara made me comfortable with the challenge ahead.

It was obvious that our team wanted to play more than one more game this time, and they set out to prove it. They pushed the four previous trips to the tournament, all of which had ended with a one and done loss, to the backs of their minds and focused on the task at hand. Led by the savvy play of our point guard Amy Vachon—along with the efforts of players Jamie Cassidy, Martina Tinklova, Kristen McCormick, and others, such as Katie Clark, Kelly Bowman, and Andrea Clark—we made history together. We played a great game and pulled off the upset, beating Stanford 60 to 58. It was the first NCAA Tournament victory in Maine's history—and a stunner. The kids were running on the floor and going crazy. Stanford literally had 12 all-Americans on their team; we had none, because Cindy had graduated the year before.

From where I was standing near our bench, I couldn't see the clock very well and wasn't really sure when the game ended. All of my assistants started jumping on me from behind; I just hoped that they were right and that the game truly was over. We were totally connected as that last shot grazed the rim. It was a moment of complete triumph, the culmination of seven years of hard work by so many people.

Unfortunately, we really did not have time to enjoy the victory. Our second game against Old Dominion would take place in less than 48 hours. We almost immediately had to shift our focus from one of exhilaration to one of preparation. Such is life in the NCAA Tournament.

Old Dominion was one of the traditional powers in women's basketball, and had a terrific coach in Wendy Larry. We had to play them on their court. It was an incredibly physical game—something we weren't accustomed to. We had our chances, and we were down by only three points with two minutes to play. Each team was called for 21 fouls, but Old Dominion was much more aggressive, and our team members were definitely not used to that style of play.

Our kids had a great tournament, and I was kind of glad to see how upset they were about losing the game. I viewed it as a sign of the progress our team had made over the previous couple of seasons. We were no longer satisfied with merely getting a spot in the tournament field. We had now experienced what it felt like to win that opening game and how much it hurt to lose a game in the second round that we honestly thought we could win.

As had been the case in some previous years, the end of our season marked the beginning of the rumor season—the time of year when people started whispering that I was leaving Maine for this school or that school. I had become somewhat immune to all of the talk, and I was so happy with everything we had accomplished during the season that I really had not even noticed which schools were going to be looking for new coaches.

Despite having listened to offers from several schools over the years, I don't think I had ever been close to saying yes to any of them. I enjoyed coaching at Maine. I loved the state; John and Maddie were happy; and we had a pretty idyllic life.

John and I had talked about the future and the fact that someday a job might come along that would force us to make a tough decision. Then, when I heard that my alma mater, Northwestern, was looking for a new coach, I knew that time just might have come.

None of the other schools I had ever talked to about a coaching vacancy had the pull on me that Northwestern did. I knew I had to at least listen to what they had to say; so I flew to Chicago to meet with athletic director Rick Taylor. John did not go with me, which I think was a sign to both of us that we were unsure about the situation. Whether I would stay or go was the hot topic in Maine for several days, but I knew in my heart what I was going to do.

I simply didn't feel the connection when Rick gave me the tour around the Northwestern campus. Nothing had changed much since I played there, which seemed odd to me. I knew what my life was like in Maine, and I knew what life in Evanston was like. It was very expensive there, and I didn't think they would be able to pay me enough to go there. I also could not see giving up my family's quality of life in Maine for what life would be like in Illinois.

I didn't say a word as Rick drove me to the airport—one of the few times in my life when this happened. I just stared straight ahead. Finally, I thanked him profusely for considering me, but let him know that there was just no way that I could say yes. It wasn't even close.

My gut told me to go back to Maine and have a heck of a year—a decision that I think made everybody happy. I signed a new five-year contract; it included pay raises for my assistants, a larger recruiting budget, and improved marketing, all of which I thought were necessary if we were going to be able to build the program to the point where it could eventually be a candidate to reach the Final Four, which was always the stated goal.

I knew the only reason I would ever leave Maine would be to go to a more established program that provided this kind of opportunity. As happy as I was there, and as much success as we had enjoyed, we still were falling short of that goal. I knew our 1999–2000 team was going to be very good; I was excited to see just *how* good.

NEW DEVELOPMENTS ON THE COURT AND IN MY LIFE

Another reason I felt good about where I was stemmed from a decision I had made a month or so after suffering my miscarriage. I had begun receiving acupuncture treatments from a woman I called

"Mother Nature," because she looked just like that mythical woman with gray hair and large, warm blue eyes.

Mary Margaret was an older woman whom my friend Terry recommended that I go see. I knew nothing about acupuncture, and wondered if it would indeed help me heal as Terry had claimed. Because she was smart enough to present the opportunity this way—encouraging me to go see her and decide whether I liked her—I was more inclined to give it a try.

I didn't think I would like it, but Mary Margaret was terrific. She got me to talk, even cry, about a lot of issues that had been on my mind, and she taught me some different ways of looking at things. She encouraged me to be a little more eager in helping myself. I learned to be less stubborn and more open to trying new ideas and ways of caring for myself and viewing myself in the world. I learned a valuable lesson from her, which was to be able to seek help from other people. You have to build a support group and find people who can help you reenergize and refocus. Mary Margaret did that for me in a very pivotal way.

Her biggest impact on my life, however, would not come for several more months, at the end of the 2000 season. It was a hectic, crazy, and confusing time. We did not play as well as either I or the team had expected, and we were struggling to put forth a consistent effort throughout a game. I still believed in the team, and was encouraged when we won 9 of 10 games in one stretch during the middle of the season. There honestly was no thought in my mind of looking into the possibility of leaving Maine.

The first call I received from Michigan State athletic director Clarence Underwood in early February caught me off guard. Their longtime coach, Karen Langeland, had announced early in the season that she was leaving after 24 years in the job. Clarence said he didn't care whether I was thinking about the job or not; he just wanted to open the lines of communication.

Dealing with a situation like this *after* the season was one thing; but there was no way I was going to let myself be distracted or sidetracked during the course of the season. Somebody once said I was the queen of one-dimensional thinking during the course of a season, and really, I believe that is what fans and players should expect from any coach.

Clarence and I hit it off right away. We came up with a plan that on my one day off a week, Michigan State representatives could call; I would not talk to them at any other point during a week.

The calls came in pretty consistently for the rest of the season, not only from Clarence but from other people, as well. The governor of Michigan, John Engler, called to ask how I was doing. Tom Izzo, the men's coach and one of the most respected coaches in our business, called me and left a message when I was unavailable.

On top of everything that was going on with our team, I had recently found out that I was pregnant again. After suffering the miscarriage a couple of years earlier, I was determined to do my best to take care of myself and give birth to a healthy baby (whom we knew was going to be a boy).

My emotions almost always get the best of me during games. During one in December at Southwest Missouri State, I thought a dubious call by the referee—with no time left on the clock—made the difference in the game. One of the best women's college players ever, Jackie Stiles, was at SMS then; she made both free throws after the foul call and we lost the game. I started yelling so loud my face got red. One of our players, Katie Clark, said she could see the vein in my neck popping out because I was so mad; she was worried about me because I was so pregnant. And even though I told the official, "You're going to make me have this baby right here," he still would not change his call.

The issue that worried me the most was whether the baby would be born before or after the end of the season, which, of course, depended in large measure on how well we played. We lost to Vermont in the championship game of the conference tournament; it was the third time they beat us that year. So our fate was once again left in the hands of the NCAA selection committee. In their ultimate wisdom, they sent us to Santa Barbara, California, to play North Carolina. I sat and watched the matchup come up on the television, and my first thought was "Are you kidding me?" I knew that pregnancy was not the NCAA's primary concern, but really? I wasn't really expecting any favors from the committee, but they had to know I was eight months pregnant, and it usually is recommended that a woman in that condition not get on an airplane, much less fly clear across the country.

My doctor admitted that he could not keep me from going (as though I would have listened if he told me to stay home). My parents offered their advice about making sure I was careful and slowing down, but nobody flat out told me I couldn't go. I tried to get a couple of friends of mine to go with me, one of whom was a midwife, but they could not clear the time on their schedules. One of our players, Tracy Guerrette, was actually a premed major; so I (only half-jokingly) told her that she was going to have to help me out if the baby decided to come at some inopportune time. I don't think she was too excited about that possibility, but she smiled her enthusiastic smile anyway.

The trip would have been difficult enough if we were flying by charter, but we were flying commercial. We had to fly from Portland to Philadelphia, change planes, fly to Los Angeles and then take a 45-minute bus ride to Santa Barbara. I did consult with the airline about its procedures if I went into labor during the flight. I was told the first step was to seek assistance from any medical people who happened to be on the plane, and if the situation reached a critical point, they would land the plane at the nearest available airport. I also had a doctor available to me in Santa Barbara who was in contact with my doctor in Maine. So, I just said a few quick prayers as I got on the plane and hoped for the best.

The flight went fine, but the bus ride was much more difficult, since the bus did not have very good shocks. I just kept hoping that the baby would hold on for a while longer. Luckily, he did.

We had some time to relax after we got to California, and one of the greatest moments I can recall about the trip was floating in the pool and talking to the cheerleaders and fans while Maddie was swimming in the pool. I was truly a whale at that point; I had gained 50 pounds, and had juice cravings, which ensured the significant weight gain. Yet it was so wonderful to relax and spend time with family, especially at the pool, which helped take away many aches and pains.

Of course, we weren't there to relax; we had a formidable opponent to face on the court. We were ahead for more than 30 minutes during the game, but the Tar Heels started playing better defensively, and, led by Nikki Teasley, they came back and eventually won.

I had more than the game on my mind, however. I was worried about getting back to Maine without having any complications with the baby—and the Michigan State job was still lurking. One of the NCAA officials who was at the regional in Santa Barbara told me that I would be a good match with MSU. I appreciated her faith, but I was surprised at the timing of her comment, which came while we were preparing to play North Carolina.

Her statement resonated with me, though. After eight years at Maine, I was seriously starting to wonder whether it was time to leave. We had made the NCAA Tournament field six times, and had lost in the first round in all but one of those years. I know I talked about going to the Final Four, but I honestly was having doubts about me being the coach who could do it. Additionally, the Michigan State people were doing a great job recruiting me. They knew about the pregnancy, of course, and how it would be almost impossible for me to visit East Lansing for an interview. So instead, seven of the school administrators flew to Portland, and John and I went there to meet them at a hotel.

I was so big and uncomfortable by that point. I recall my first introduction to Clarence Underwood from Michigan State: When I turned around to meet him, my stomach smacked right into him. It broke the ice immediately, making our first encounter very intimate and very humorous.

The administrators asked questions, and the more we talked, the more John and I just knew this was the right time to make a move. I had to literally take a deep breath every time I tried to answer a question because the baby was pushing against my diaphragm. The longer the interview lasted, the less breath I had.

I knew that my team and I had accomplished a great deal at Maine, a lot more than I think the university could have anticipated when it hired a 26-year-old assistant with very limited experience. I felt good about where we had taken the program, how we had achieved more recognition, and how we had closed the gap that had existed between the women's team and some of the men's sports programs. I felt particularly proud that we had recruited some amazing talent, which would be at Maine for years to come, in players like Julie Vevilleux, Heather Ernst, and Melissa Heon. I knew that Maine's future was very bright—with or without my leadership. My philosophy truly was that I wanted to leave wherever I had been better than I had found it; I knew the Maine program was in much better shape than when I had taken over as coach, and I felt good about that. I would have felt worse had I thought I was leaving the cupboard bare, but the team had some great players, with more outstanding recruits coming.

Michigan State and I agreed on a five-year contract, and I accepted the job as the head coach of the Spartans without ever seeing East Lansing. It was a package deal, as John was told he would also receive a full-time job teaching economics.

Transitioning from one job to another is never easy. Even though I was excited about the new opportunity and knew in my heart it was the right decision, I still had to say good-bye to a lot of people who had meant a lot to me, both personally and professionally. Meeting with the team was extremely difficult; there really is not much anyone can say after you tell people that you're leaving them. The meeting I had with the team in the locker room was fairly brief. We held a news conference, and then I went back to my office to pack up some things before I headed home.

It was a little before 4:00 PM, and I was exhausted. By this time, we knew the baby was going to be a boy, whom we would name John Wyatt (Jack, for short). Even though I was excited about going to Michigan State, I still was sad and down about leaving Maine. As I drove home, I whispered to Jack that everything was okay now— that he could come whenever he was ready.

Saying that seemed to give me a sense of relief, and I really meant it. All of the stress was now behind us, and I could give my full atten-tion to Jack. When I arrived home at about 4:00 PM, I told John and Maddie that the first thing I wanted to do was take a nap.

I suppose that Jack had waited long enough, because, not 20 min-utes later, my water broke. As though the day had not been dramatic enough already, I was now on the way to the hospital to give birth to an eight-pound nine-ounce baby boy.

I really didn't know whether I had the strength to get through it. I had gained more weight with Jack (close to 50 pounds) than with Maddie. I was incredibly emotionally wrung out, and I knew the birth was not going to be easy. Though I was determined to have a natural childbirth, I was in a lot of pain and thought something might be wrong. I told the delivery room nurse that I just didn't think I could do it. Jack's birth was complicated further by the fact that he became stuck. There was discussion about doing a C-section, but I didn't want to do it. The baby's heart rate was dropping, and I was emotionally, physically, and mentally spent.

The nurse grabbed me by the collar very aggressively, and got right in my face. "You get him out *now*," she yelled, emphasizing the last word, and I gave my big push as she said "now." I was not going to say no to this woman. She was a true coach herself; she found that extra energy in me and drew it forth. I was crying, and I still didn't think I could do it, but this nurse pulled me through. I could never have done it without her, and I told her that after it was all over a few hours later. A great coach can propel you forward even during your weakest moments. This woman did that for me, and became one of the greatest coaches I have ever had—even though I don't even remember her name. She made a difference for me at a crucial moment.

The message, I think, for any new mother is to understand that you are not Superwoman. I had really pushed the envelope with Jack in a completely different way than I had done with Maddie, and I was just happy and grateful that he was a healthy baby. I was determined not to make the same mistakes that I had made with Maddie. I knew I was going to stay home with him for a month, and I did, even though Clarence Underwood, my new boss, kept calling me every day asking when I would be moving to East Lansing. I told him I was doing what I needed to do from home, and that I would not be there for a month. I could always tell that Clarence was smiling at the other end of the phone, and he kept saying that they were anxious to introduce me in person, because people in East Lansing were beginning to wonder whether I really existed and whether the school had really hired me as the head coach. But that one month off was pivotal for me—and one of the most enjoyable months of my life.

Before leaving Maine, I did go back to my "Mother Nature" for a final acupuncture treatment. Yet much more important to me than the treatment was what she told me that day. She told me that Maine was a "granite" state, and that granite is a rock. In contrast, I was a "fire-starter," she said rather simply, and that rock puts out fire. She told me I needed to leave; that if I didn't, my fire would be put out. In her view, it was time for me to take the next step.

I asked her what Michigan was made of, and she smiled, paused, and said, "*Sand*. You will have the time of your life," she promised. With her big blue eyes of wisdom, she told me, "You were made for sand and water."

I was not about to disagree.

The McCallie family—Jack, John, Joanne, and Maddie—during the summer of 2010 at Bald Head Island, North Carolina, taking time to reenergize.
Source: Personal Collection

CHAPTER 9 QUESTIONS

- Balancing the different aspects in your life is accomplished by prioritizing. Do you manage your priorities well?
- How do you care for others in times of need?
- How do you prepare for success in your professional and personal life? Are you comfortable with success?
- Longevity and success over time can be exhausting. How do you reenergize and heal in your life presently?
- Success generates new opportunities. How do you handle opportunity when it appears?
- Do you recognize the daily heroes in your life?

10

SET HIGH TEAM GOALS WHILE MOTIVATING ON AN INDIVIDUAL LEVEL

NO TWO PLAYERS (JUST LIKE NO TWO EMPLOYEES) ARE EXACTLY ALIKE

ARRIVING AT MICHIGAN STATE

I was excited and energized about the challenge of coaching at Michigan State; however, I knew that my first priority after saying yes to the job was taking care of Jack. I was determined not to make some of the mistakes I had made after Maddie was born, primarily not rushing immediately back to working full-time.

My eight years of head coaching experience at Maine made me much more comfortable in transitioning to Michigan State. I was confident in my abilities to coach, and I knew what was involved in rebuilding a program. I knew I would feel comfortable coaching in the Big Ten because of my experience playing in the league myself. I was familiar with the schools and the towns; I didn't see my move to East Lansing as anything less than a tremendous opportunity.

As any couple that has gone through a job change and relocation knows, this is not a simple process. Once again, however, I had the advantage of being married to a great husband who took care of most of the details. While I was home recuperating in the month after Jack was born, John and his great friend, Stan Bagley, went to East Lansing, found us a house, bought it, and arranged our move. I didn't even see a picture of it, but I had that kind of faith and trust in John. This was an example of the confidence John had in himself, as well as a testament to his ability to get a lot done at once, since he also had time to fit in 18 holes of golf on the same day he bought our house.

Some women I know would not be comfortable having their husband take care of such a big decision as buying a house, but that was how much confidence I had in John. I knew he would find us the perfect home in a wonderful neighborhood, and that is exactly what he did.

With our housing issues taken care of, I was able to concentrate on the fact that I was coming to Michigan State at an exciting time. The women's basketball team had won 19 games the previous year and finished in the middle of the Big Ten. The men's team had just won the NCAA championship under coach Tom Izzo, which created an enormous amount of excitement and interest in the program.

I knew that the success of the men's team could only help us as we set out to upgrade the women's program. We were getting new facilities that would be as good as those of any university in the country, and I was getting the chance to work with and learn from Tom, one of the truly great coaches in the United States. I wanted to expose our players to that, and I wanted them to see what it was like to win a National Championship. I wanted them to appreciate how hard Tom and his players worked, to realize that all of the sacrifices were worth it when you won. Having that National Championship trophy on display was a motivator for me. I was very honest when I told both the team and the media: "We want one of those."

I never thought twice about setting high goals for myself and our team. I think I would have been doing a disservice to our players and to our fans if I had made our goals to win the Big Ten championship, or to qualify for the NCAA Tournament. Although we could have accomplished these feats more easily, nobody involved in our program would have been satisfied by doing so.

There were some points early in my time at Michigan State when I suspect Tom didn't know quite what to make of me. Yet it was obvious to me from day one that Tom and his assistants (Brian Gregory, a dear friend and now the head coach at Georgia Tech, and Mike Garland) could be valuable assets for me and our team. I immediately saw that I would be missing a great opportunity if I didn't take advantage of their knowledge and experience. As I'd done so many times before, I was jumping at the chance to learn from those who had reached the goals I set for myself and my team. I was so excited and motivated to hear about their climb to the top.

I'd always been eager to learn from others' experiences. It started back when I was that kid in high school who was just not afraid to ask questions. I took that belief with me to Northwestern, then on to Auburn and Maine, and I didn't see any reason to stop now. It also made even more sense to me to stick close to Tom as much as possible, because he had been so successful and had won the national title. He had done what I wanted to do, and that's why I wanted to be around him. I knew it would be important for me to surround myself with people who had been where I wanted to go.

Tom knew the challenges that the women's team faced, which I think was one reason he was so helpful to and cooperative with me in those early years. He knew that I wasn't a threat to him or his program in any way. I really appreciated how he invited me to donor events at his house, so I could get to know some of the important people and boosters of the men's program and to view practice whenever it was convenient.

Tom was a great mentor to me; I'll probably never be able to thank him properly for the access he gave me to his program, for answering all of my questions, and for involving me in the process of building our new facilities. We got to pick out the carpet, the office furniture, and all of the other equipment, which gave us as fine a facility as any team in the country. Tom even helped me deal with an academic situation involving a struggling student who had gotten into some problems and needed support. He understood the value of support when taking a program to the next level. His direction and insights were simply invaluable.

LESSONS FROM TOM IZZO AND LONNY ROSEN

What I truly learned from my years with Tom was how to be a better coach. I watched and listened to him, and applied what I learned to coaching my own players.

I describe Tom as a "blue-collar coach" because his teams are so rough and physical. That is the way you have to play to win in the Big Ten, due to the perpetual battle in the paint. His teams have a quality of grittiness that I respect—a quality I wanted to consistently see in my own players.

When you still consider yourself a student in whatever occupation you happen to be in, it is only natural to want to seek the opinions and advice of those around you who have had more experience—those who have achieved the success that you are trying to achieve. I had never had that chance at Maine, and having it when I came to Michigan almost left me feeling like a kid in a candy store. What were the keys to Tom's success? What was the process required to win a national title? How do you get to the next level after accomplishing the first title?

Though I don't know exactly what Tom thought when I asked him if I could come to his practices to watch, he agreed to let me do it. Since I wanted to respect his space, I didn't go to every practice. I attended when I could, took notes, and tried to implement what I learned into our own practices. I leaned on him when I needed him, and quickly began to consider him as a big brother figure. He came to some of our games, and was very supportive of women's basketball in his public comments.

Some of the lessons I learned from Tom that really helped me improve as a coach and our girls improve as a team included elements such as the physical nature of his practices, as well as lessons on how to navigate Michigan State for administrative support, guidance, and exposure to some of the people who were key to the success of our program. There were so many little things that I picked up by watching Tom coach during games and practices—and I learned even more by observing him during the recruiting process. He was an invaluable asset to our program.

I really give Tom a lot of credit for including us, and for his desire to see the women's program grow and develop. He never felt threatened by our success—and why should he? Tom was secure with his situation; he had no reason to not want me and our team to be successful. I know that some men's coaches might not have been so helpful and generous, which is why I feel especially lucky to have had Tom as a colleague.

One of the most important things Tom showed me was to completely change the way I studied film after watching and talking with him. I hired a film expert named Paul Rivers who knew Tom, and we began to break down film the exact same way the men's team did. Paul worked with our team for a year, and then went to work for Tom.

I was happy to share Paul with the men's basketball team. He was so professional and efficient that I knew his long-term desire was to be on the men's side, and then the pros. All of that was okay with me, because I love helping people get where they want to be. It was another lesson to me that applies not just to basketball, but to countless other positions or scenarios in life and in business. You have to learn where and when you can help guide and enhance the career directions of those who work with you.

Another person who came into my life soon after I arrived in East Lansing has had a tremendous impact on me over the years: Dr. Lonny Rosen, a psychiatry professor at Michigan State. I can't remember how or when I met Lonny, as he came into my life very quietly and gently. I discovered that he was an expert in sports psychiatry, and he quickly became a friend and teacher. I have always felt that Lonny is someone who can explain things to me so all of the facts make sense.

Though Lonny looks like a mad scientist, with a beard and gray hair, intense eyes, and intimidating knowledge, I found his presence kind of reassuring. He explained his job and abilities to me, and offered his assistance whenever my team or I needed help—and I fell in love with his mind and problem-solving ability. I could tell almost immediately that he was going to become a tremendous resource for my team and me. I have known him for about 11 years now, and I'm still learning from his process-driven thinking.

Lonny has taught me how to develop a better understanding of how to motivate each player individually. He emphasizes that it's best not to coach with or to have a fan or scoreboard mentality, and he has trained me to respond effectively to both success and failure. Most important, Lonny trained me to establish and maintain high standards for my program. He showed me how small verbal cues and motivators could make handling relationships with the players much more personal and effective.

One of the best things Lonny did for our program took place a couple of years after I had arrived in East Lansing. We had recruited a point guard named Kristin Haynie who came down with mononucleosis during her sophomore year. She was very sick, and none of the doctors could figure out what the problem was and why she wasn't getting better.

It was Lonny who figured out what was wrong after Kristin shared with him the fact that she had undergone surgery to remove some polyps on her intestine when she was 11 years old. Lonny discerned that Kristin's doctors had essentially removed her large intestine during the procedure, and that this was preventing her body from absorbing enough nutrients. She had no energy, and she simply couldn't get better.

Lonny figured out that Kristin needed to consume about 4,000 calories a day for her body to absorb the appropriate nutrients. Though Kristin was a very quiet and shy girl, Lonny was able to talk to her, explain why she was not improving, and convince her to do what she had to do to get better. Once that happened, it taught me to have an incredible appreciation for Lonny's craft. It has been gratifying to stay in contact with him through the years.

Many of the talks I had with Lonny had nothing to do with basketball or my team. We often ended up discussing human activity and trying to determine the best way to motivate individuals. I've found that the ability to encourage players is the most telling factor in a coach's success or failure, which is another reason Lonny and I became so close. His ideas are always one notch above the common thinker. His world is very clear; it's not abstract, but his keen sense of causal relationships and events helped me simplify my coaching to a wonderful process of getting better, and living and attacking dangerously with my teams. Everyone in sports or business needs to seek out and find a "Lonny" in their world. Wisdom connected with experience, fueled by an incredible mutual appreciation for each other's roles, makes for great growth and overall development.

MOTIVATING A NEW TEAM

I have always believed that motivating on an individual level is absolutely necessary to get more out of a team than the talent level would normally produce. A player has to believe in you—and you have to believe in the player—if you are going to reach the highest level possible and have the team as a whole rise to meet the occasion.

That philosophy works in business as well. The best leaders and executives are the ones who are able to get the greatest effort and production out of their employees. They do so through motivation, and by realizing that no two employees—just like no two players—are exactly alike. What works to inspire one person can fall flat with somebody else, and vice versa. The best leaders are the ones who are able to recognize and adjust their philosophies to deal with each individual, while keeping every member of their team focused on the same goal.

Coaches and bosses have to be willing to seek the truth and share themselves if they want to find out what drives each of their players or employees. An element of trust must exist on both sides in order for a relationship between a coach and a player (or a boss and an employee) to develop and thrive.

When a school, or a even professional team, hires a new coach, a period of adjustment always has to occur. The players don't know the coach, the coach doesn't know the players, and there is a natural "feeling-out" phase. As with any new employee who starts a job, connections must be made—and habits must be established—in order to get the ball rolling.

I was passionate about making this kind of a natural transition and trying to move forward daily. I was able to do this more effectively at Duke because of what I experienced in my early time at Michigan State. I would advise any business leader moving into a role similar to that of a new coach in the following way: There needs to be a lot of one-on-one meetings between the coach and players (or the boss and employees) wherein everyone present is given the chance to discuss everything they want to discuss. There doesn't need to be an agenda, but it's best to spend some time talking and answering team members' questions. Leaders need to learn what is important and valuable to the people they're managing—to discover what drives them and makes them want to do their best.

I've also found it worthwhile to spend some nonworking, social time with my team members. I will occasionally invite them for meals at my house, so that they can get to know me and my family, too. I also chose to start an informal program at Duke called "walk the dog." During these meetings, I had each team member come over to my house independently and go for a walk with me and our dog Kibo. This really provided a great opportunity for me to talk about a lot of different things and to get to know each of my players as individuals. The most critical thing I learned was that the players wanted to know that their coach was interested in them, and they wanted me to make an effort to get to know them as quickly as possible.

You have to establish your staff, your team members, and the auxiliary people around your program. You must decide whether you are going to rehire some of the people who were already there and who you are going to bring in from the outside. I'm not crazy about the phrase "keeping people on" when referring to employees who previously worked with the program. I think it's better to say they were "rehired" by the new coach, because that's who they are working for now, and that's where their loyalty needs to be. Everybody involved in the program has to immediately support you and your philosophy, and you have to interact with all of these individuals as much as possible. The rehire process is an attempt to show value to all—wherever they worked in the past.

New coaches and leaders must also realize that, as much as you might want to, you can't rush the process. There is no way you can earn immediate trust, or have people begin caring for each other right away. In order for this to be genuine, it has to happen gradually and naturally. Any newly appointed leader has to be careful to avoid creating a phony environment for the sake of everyone getting along. A situation where relationships and actions have passed the test of time—and where members have shared experiences—is far more valuable in the long run.

I have never understood how people can claim that coaches can't succeed until they get "their own" players on the team, meaning players a coach has personally recruited and signed. This attitude bothers me; it sends the message that I can't work and succeed with the players who were already there when I got there. Transitions work much more effectively when the leader's actions show that he or she would have chosen everyone there, even those who came before.

Experiencing a coaching change as a player at Northwestern helped me understand what players expect and are looking for when a new coach takes over. I also believe that after months of practice and enduring an entire season together, those players are no longer part of the former coach's team. They are now *my* players, and part of *my* team. Bumpy times can occur during this period, as it's often wrought with baggage and issues resulting from change. You have to stay on course and remain principled, which is of course easier said than done.

Many people used to take the general attitude that a new coach is on somewhat of a honeymoon period when they take over a program. However, that's not really the case anymore. A new coach is always met with high expectations from the start, along with a big dollar commitment from the school. Because of the money coaches are paid, the school and boosters want immediate results, so there is a lot of pressure for a coach to hit the ground running.

New head coaches have to understand that their clock begins ticking the second they arrive at a school. They have to produce success within three or four years, or their contracts aren't likely to be renewed. I was coming to Michigan State to build a successful program; while I knew it would be important how we played in our first season, I also remembered how hard that first season had been at Maine. I was not going to become discouraged or depressed if we struggled in the 2000–2001 season, as long as I saw a clear improvement evolving.

One of the most rewarding feelings as a coach arises when you believe the players buy into your program, and truly "get" what you are saying. One of our first goals as a team that first season at Michigan State was to get physically stronger and to raise the intensity level of our practices—something I knew would translate into increased intensity during games. I was looking for commitment and renewal from the players, as well as the realization that there was a clean slate for everybody. Some players literally thrive when a new coach shows up; they simply find a freedom with a new coach that they had not experienced before.

I wanted the level of intensity I embraced to rub off on the players, and I think it did. I think the players could tell that I was not fake at all, which would have turned them off very quickly, but entirely sincere and genuine instead. Getting up at 5:30 AM to lift weights is not easy for anybody, especially college students, but it was necessary if we were going to get stronger physically. We had a corps of five seniors, and I really was counting on them to set an example and lead the way for the younger players.

One of the ways we worked to get stronger was by playing against a male team who had all played high school basketball. I knew those practices would be harder and more physically challenging than our actual games in many ways, but that was okay with me. We got stronger and more intense, which was the goal.

What we struggled with, however, was individual performance consistency. We used 10 different starting lineups during our first 16 games. I was trying to let my team know that I could not tolerate a lack of productivity and that a player had to *earn* her spot in the starting lineup. Changing the lineup generates a new energy among the team. People feel a sense of power when they believe that they can change their situation. If a player believes that she is destined to be on the bench forever, then she will very likely lose any sense of power or confidence. Having players who feel that way does not create the level of energy needed to develop a team that is pursuing championships annually.

Coaches and business leaders cannot be afraid of change, because change can show and teach you things about your team that you never knew before. There is almost always a positive effect as a result of altering something. Some coaches stick with the same starting lineup as a kind of security blanket. Though I also love such consistency, it has to be warranted. Knowing when to make a change, and what change to make, is the art of being a good leader and motivator.

Much like my first season at Maine, in my first year at MSU, we lost way too many games, and we ended up being only 4 and 12 in the Big Ten. We lost nine consecutive conference games during one disappointing stretch. I was disappointed, because I wanted us to be more successful right away; however, I had to keep reminding myself to remain patient. We were changing a culture and building a program—and even though immediate results would have been enjoyable, we had more important long-term goals. Still, it never feels good to struggle when expectations and desires are so much higher than one's current situation. We all felt pressure to be better.

MANAGING CONFLICT

One of the realities of coaching is that you never know when something you say to your players is going to register with them—and you never know how they are going to react to certain situations. Every player—just as every employee or person in an organization—is different. Therefore, coaches and bosses face the challenge of learning how to motivate and inspire each of those people individually and how to get the most out of their abilities collectively, thereby making the team or company as good as it can be for the long term.

When a coach or a boss comes into a new school or company from somewhere else, everyone has to take some time to adjust. The players need to know what makes the coach tick, and the coach has to learn all about the players. This occurs with all new players in any year, but the experience and history you have built up with the older players is important so that they can help to educate the new ones.

One of the points that I try to emphasize most is that every player, every person, has his or her own set of assumptions, and everyone's point of view is different. It's as simple as two circles to me: *situation* and *person*. I try to have my players and staff understand the difference between these two by asking them, "Are you capable of evaluating your situation, or do you view everything personally?"

It almost always seems personal, of course, when I have trouble with team members or someone on my staff. Their personal baggage from former employers and/or family challenges in the past tends to come into play, and I end up hearing statements like, "Coach, you don't trust me. Coach, you don't like me." This social, psychological principle of person versus situation can therefore go a long way in simplifying communication and getting to the heart of the situational conflict. This understanding is a means to producing clarity quickly—to bringing forth the "situation" and removing the emotional baggage that can stop people from growing.

The key is to get all those involved to examine their role through a "situation" lens. What things do they control? How can they improve? "Personal" interpretations lead only to confusion and a "victim mentality," whereby they lose their individual power and often engage in blaming—rather than in claiming responsibility.

This really is a fundamental underpinning of the right thinking and "Choice Not Chance" philosophy. When a player claims to not understand me, she is invariably stuck in "personal" thinking, and I have to get her out. I have actually found that it helps to draw actual pictures—a technique I use in staff reviews and during one-on-one meetings with the players. I use circles, diagrams, whatever it takes, to show where we are versus where we need to be.

By the time I started my second year at Michigan State, I felt pretty good about the relationships I had established with our players and the new recruits we had signed. The fact that we were moving into our new facilities also had everyone around the program excited.

We had a great nonconference season and won 9 of 10 games before we opened the Big Ten season with losses to Indiana and Michigan. We had one more nonconference game to play; it was at home against Georgia, who was undefeated and ranked eighth in the country at the time. It was also going to be nationally televised by CBS.

We were in the film room preparing for Georgia a day or so before the game when one player said something that caused another player to react angrily, and before long, two of the players were in a scuffle. Even though I saw it coming, I decided to let it go and let the girls work it out on their own. Since it was not a situation that I thought would become dangerous, I walked out of the room. I know that a lot of coaches would have reacted differently and instinctively tried to break up the fight. However, I felt that such tension was necessary in order for us to grow and take on an undefeated team, especially one against whom we matched up very poorly at all five positions. Learning maturity and accountability was something we needed very badly at this time.

I couldn't sleep the whole night before the game; I was constantly thinking about it, and almost playing the game in my mind. When I got to our shooting practice the next morning, I heard the team screaming in the locker room, playing really loud music, and carrying on in a silly way. I asked what they were doing, and they said they were getting ready for the game. I knew they were nervous and over-reacting at the wrong time. Many immature athletes can forget the appropriate time and place to do what they need to do. The five hours before game time should be spent on shooting practice, a pregame meal, and quiet time—not by wasting valuable energy or taking time to "hype it up," which is typically done immediately before tip-off.

I was very calm when I told them they needed to settle down, and they all looked at me kind of funny. I told them they needed to recognize the fact that they were very nervous about the upcoming game. The locker room became very still, and the music came down while the players stood and looked at me. I told them to all take a deep breath and focus on what we were going to be doing that night. "It's going to be a great night," I said, and walked out of the locker room.

There is no book to teach this to a coach; it is simply a combination of instinct and experience. We had plenty of challenging games against terrific opponents during my time at Maine, so I had seen this kind of behavior before—players mistaking nervous, silly hype for focus. A coach has to have enough intuition, knowledge, and experience to know that having your players waste all of that energy won't serve you well. In an effort to turn the nervousness into something more positive, I asked one of the team leaders if we were good now. "Real good," she said. This allowed the team to understand how much I believed in them.

After this interaction, we went out and upset Georgia by 21 points on national television. I attribute much of the credit for the win to the fight that took place beforehand—and the team's ability to handle such internal adversity, along with the true fear factor of wondering whether we could beat them. We never talked about the incident again. But it just goes to show that even conflict can serve a purpose sometimes.

Knowing when to speak up and talk about a situation versus when to keep your mouth shut is one of those intangible skills that good leaders just naturally possess. You certainly can't take a class that teaches you how to do it, yet it might be one of the most valuable traits a leader can possess, and I do think you can learn to be better at it. I know that the more I've coached, the more at ease I've come to feel in talking to my players about issues not even remotely associated with basketball.

Having players open up to me, and my being able to communicate with them as well, has truly fostered healthy relationships between us. Players who are afraid of or reluctant to admit to their coach that they have problems are probably not going to communicate very well with the other players on the court, either. Teams that get along well off the court generally are more successful than teams that bicker; however, there are always exceptions to that rule. Understanding and respecting other players is probably more important than anything else.

Any good leader (whether a coach, a boss, or someone else) must realize that there are going to be team members who just don't get along—for whatever reason. Personalities and preferences differ, and sometimes they clash in ways that just cannot be helped. I faced such a scenario at Michigan State with two of our star players, Kristin Haynie and Lindsay Bowen, who were a year apart in school.

Kristin and Lindsay had been rivals in high school; I knew they had some strong feelings about each other when we were recruiting them, and I felt that they had to deal with those feelings. I told the girls that what had happened in high school was in the past; though they may have butted heads, college was different and much more competitive. I told Lindsay specifically that while she could certainly think whatever she wanted about any opposing player, the conflict had to stop when they put on the same uniform and started playing for the same team.

I gave Lindsay the following advice: "You are going to laugh, mature, and look back on high school as a funny time—because you are going to be on a different level and see things in a totally different way during your college years." I think the two girls did become close as they spent more time together; in fact, they ended up being the most dynamic backcourt duo in the history of Michigan State women's basketball together. Since Lindsay was one year younger, she had to have the vision to join Kristin as a Spartan. She did—something for which so many people are grateful.

We were making progress. I could feel it and see it.

Coach P coaching her team during the 2009 Caribbean Challenge in Cancún, Mexico.
Source: Lindy Brown

11

Everybody Has to Be Challenged to See How Good They Can Become

CHALLENGES AND PROGRESS
AT MICHIGAN STATE

Unfortunately, most people see a team's success (or failure) solely in terms of wins and losses. Using these parameters, I had a disappointing second year at Michigan State.

However, we managed to play well enough to get an invitation to the WNIT Tournament. Even though it was not as coveted as a spot in the NCAA Tournament, I still viewed it as a sign that we were making progress. It also allowed us to keep practicing and playing games.

A victory over DePaul in the first round moved us into the second round at Illinois, where we won again. We hosted Alabama in the quarterfinals and won, which sent us to Oregon for the semifinal game against the Ducks, where, unfortunately, we lost. Though it's always disappointing to lose your final game of the year, I was pleased with how far we had come, and was already excited about our prospects for the 2002–2003 season.

It was a happy time in our personal lives. John had been hired as a full-time professor in the Economics Department and was enjoying his work. The kids were growing up and making friends. We lived in a great house in a friendly neighborhood and had become close to many people. I had once again developed friendships with some older women whom I saw as my unofficial advisers club. These people helped me through more tough situations than they will ever know.

One of my greatest sources of sadness about being at Michigan State was that I could not share my success with my college boyfriend, Tim, who had died of a brain tumor at the too-young age of 42. Michigan State had been Tim's school; his parents had moved to East Lansing, and Tim had always educated me on the difference between Michigan State and rival Michigan when we were in school at Northwestern. I was therefore well aware of the history and relationship between the two schools when I got to East Lansing.

Being at Michigan State did give me the chance to meet and get to know some really fascinating people. One of the greatest basketball players ever, Magic Johnson, is a Michigan State alum, and he would show up from time to time for different events. Of course, since I had grown up a fan of the Boston Celtics, my favorite player was Larry Bird. He had been Johnson's biggest rival ever since Michigan State and Indiana State met for the NCAA championship in 1979 (a classic game in the history of college basketball). I chose 33 as my uniform number in college because of Larry Bird.

We were in the auxiliary gym having practice one day when I happened to see a tall man who I did not immediately recognize standing at the other end of the second court. I had seen Magic walking through the gym earlier in the practice. Though I had no idea he was in town until that moment, that really wasn't a big deal (as strange as that may sound!). He came around occasionally; we would say hello, talk briefly, and then he'd leave. This time was different, though, because I saw another tall man with blond hair standing there with a young girl to whom he was talking. I was very focused on what we were doing in practice; yet the longer this man stood there, the more I began to focus on him because he was so tall. Finally, he walked over and introduced his daughter and then himself. It was, of course, the one and only Larry Bird.

I was reminded at that moment of the statement I made when I started coaching at MSU; I told our players, "You are going to be the kind of team that is *entirely focused*. I don't care if the president of the United States walks into our practice; you will not be distracted. You will be playing hard and having a great time." I had established from the very beginning that we did not stop practice for *any* celebrity who happened to show up. We simply were not going to play that gawking game. I was going to respect their privacy and have them respect ours.

But this was different. This was *Larry Bird*. We shook hands, and he actually started talking about golf. The team continued practicing while we talked, and, much to their credit, didn't stop once. I finally signaled to the ladies to come over and say hi to Mr. Bird, who, it turned out, was there to coach Magic in a celebrity All-Star game. Talk about an incredible experience—unannounced, random visits from Magic Johnson and Larry Bird on the same day.

We did not play as well in the nonconference portion of the season, but got better as the year went along and finished in a tie for fourth in the Big Ten with a 10 and 6 record. That was good enough for us to be invited back to the NCAA Tournament, thereby putting an end to my two-year absence and signaling the first time the Spartans had been there since the 1996–1997 season.

Accomplishing that goal was a good feeling. We had worked hard and come together as a team, and I felt that we had truly earned the number eight seed and a first-round matchup against Texas Christian University. And even though we lost the game, this was a critical time for our program. We were learning how to be physical and how to dictate the pace of the game. It was a hard-fought game, but I think it showed us how to fight and perform in tough circumstances. It was definitely part of the process that would lead us to success in 2005.

As with the many first-round losses we had experienced at Maine, I was disappointed because I knew we could have won. This realization reinforced my belief that the only way you can improve (and to keep measuring how far you have improved) is by pitting yourself against the best and seeing how you match up.

I was incredibly happy about the fact that we had restored some of the pride in the women's basketball program at Michigan State. People now expected us to compete for a spot in the tournament every year, which was one of my goals when I took the job. Now we had to do better than that, and I thought that our 2003–2004 team was capable of making that happen.

We won 9 of our first 10 nonconference games, losing only to Oklahoma State, and moved into the national rankings in the twenty-fourth spot in early December. I try not to get too hung up on rankings, but I did view it in our case as a reward for the progress our program had made. It seemed to be a sign that others were recognizing what a good job we were doing, because it was the first time the Michigan State women had been in the top 25 national rankings since the 1996–1997 season.

That was really the point in the season when I became able to teach our players the right way of thinking about the national polls, which I called "beauty pageants." The kids thought that was funny, and I told them it was because the polls really were an expression of what the voters thought of us—based on opinion, not facts, just like the judges in a beauty pageant. You win or lose in a beauty pageant based on what others think of you. That mentality is important to teach at the beginning of a season, especially to a team that enjoys success early on. I took great care about making certain our team looked at these issues with the right frame of mind.

As soon as I compared the polls to a beauty pageant, our kids did not care one bit about them, because they sure as heck did not want to be in a beauty pageant. That was one of the fundamental critical reasons we made it to the National Championship game in 2005: We already were preparing for and managing what others thought about us with a sense of humor, and on our own terms.

Always Measure Your Accomplishments

It is important to the success of any business or company (as well as to individuals) to have ways to measure your accomplishments. This was how I viewed the rankings and the Big Ten standings. We were well aware of the challenges that still lay ahead of us, and we knew which teams we'd have to beat if we wanted to keep improving. Sometimes a business's goals and challenges are not as obvious as they are to a basketball team; however, they are there, and you will find them if you look for them. Everybody has to be pushed, and to push themselves, to see how good they can become; anybody who doesn't bother to do so will likely have a hard time finding success.

I am an upbeat coach who loves to stir the pot. I adore kids who want to compete and challenge themselves by playing against formidable rivals. Whether in athletics or business, you are only as good as those with whom you surround yourself. This is the thrust of the Choice Not Chance philosophy: *You* are responsible for the people around you, especially those with whom you choose to compete.

We had a young team featuring five freshmen and two sophomores, who were eager to learn and excited about improving. We went 10 and 6 in the conference and became the first Michigan State team since 1996–1997 to win 20 games in a season. We won our first Big Ten Tournament game since 1999, but then ran into Penn State in the conference semifinals. We were awarded an at-large bid to the NCAA

Tournament and sent to Austin, Texas, where Arizona was our first-round opponent.

A year earlier, we had been a bubble team, uncertain about whether we would get into the NCAA Tournament. Though there was little doubt this year, stranger things have happened. But regardless of how far we got, I was happy for the kids because I knew how hard they had worked. I also knew that this latest achievement meant we had made more progress as a program.

I was excited about our first-round matchup against Arizona; we won the game and moved into a second-round matchup against Texas, where we fell short of reaching the Sweet 16 for the first time. I was disappointed, but energized for the future; our young team signaled the probability of better days ahead.

One of those days came for me during the summer of 2004. My husband John was part of a group, which included Michigan State football coach John L. Smith, that climbed Mount Kilimanjaro—something that made me incredibly happy and proud. John's been an adventurer and an outdoorsman since I first met him, so I knew that this special opportunity was something he absolutely loved.

I was so tickled that John had signed on for the trip that it was all I could think about, even in the busy recruiting month of July. Being home alone with the kids was a challenge, of course; but John's success on the climb really brought a sense of power to me, too. The experience changed him and gave him a new perspective. Though John and I have had many wonderful trips together, it's important for people in relationships to realize that there also is a time to separate and give your spouse space. Both you and your spouse will grow from these experiences.

It also was a glorious time for me; while I normally would have been off recruiting, John's absence gave me the chance to stay home with my kids and just be a mom. After John got home from Tanzania, he took Maddie and Jack and went out to buy a dog, surprising me in the process. The newest member of our family was a lab puppy with light yellowish eyes and a wonderful spirit. We named him Kibo, for Kibo Hut atop Kilimanjaro, and his spirit and nature gave all of us a very good feeling heading into the season.

John was excited about his trip, and I was refreshed and ready for the next season, and our next challenge, to begin. John had climbed his mountain; now it was our team's turn.

The 2011 Duke women's basketball team onstage receiving their ACC Championship Trophy following a 66 to 58 win in the 2011 ACC Championship Game against North Carolina.
Source: Duke Photography

CHAPTER 11 QUESTIONS

- You are always meeting new people in life. How do you respond?
- What elements of a "bucket list" have you pursued in your life? What things do you still desire to pursue?
- How do you measure success in your professional and personal life?
- Do you ever care about "rankings"?

12

STEP BACK AND REASSESS YOUR PRIORITIES

HOW CAN WE IMPROVE?
WHAT CAN WE DO BETTER?

Any doubts I had about how good we were going to be in the 2004–2005 season were erased in December. First came a game at Notre Dame, and three weeks later we played at University of Connecticut.

There are really very few games after which a coach can simply sit back and view as a piece of art. We pretty much tear every game apart when we watch film afterward, win or lose, since we're always looking for ways that we can do better. Honesty is key when we are in film and require each individual to abandon their own sensitivity to allow growth for the individual players and the team. A team very rarely plays a perfect game—and even when they do, most coaches are reluctant to admit it or the team will (at least subconsciously) relax and possibly let their guard down during the next game.

The Notre Dame game in South Bend was our sixth of the season, and the Irish were ranked third in the country. We had won four of our first five games, losing only to TCU in the Rainbow Classic in Hawaii; however, we already had some hurdles to overcome. The first player I recruited when I came to Michigan State, Candice Jackson (who was now working as our graduate assistant) lost her father just as we were getting ready to leave for Hawaii. We literally had just gotten on the plane when I got the news, so there was no way I could go to his funeral. Larry Jackson was a great man and a very special person, and I felt so sorry for Candice because I knew how much she was hurting. As I had so many times before, I felt torn in my desire to be in more than one place at once. This can be especially painful, since the players sometimes don't understand the uneven balance of priorities. They often aren't aware of coaches' schedules or all of their commitments; they might assume that a coach who misses practice or a game doesn't care. They don't always recognize the many conflicts inherent in coaches' (as well as other professionals') daily lives.

No matter what profession you are in, there are moments in your life that make you step back and reassess your priorities. Losing a parent is tough at any age, but it is especially difficult for someone as young as a college student. I knew I was not going to be able to replace Larry in Candice's life, but I wanted to make sure that I was there for her and available to her as a mentor figure anytime she needed one. I really felt as though Larry's spirit and support stayed with us the entire season.

A coach–player relationship in any sport, especially at the college level, differs from the other kinds of boss–employee relationships in the business world. Professional individuals tend to be very protective of their privacy and their emotions; they often develop a bunker mentality, wherein they keep their private lives entirely to themselves. This seems like a mistake to me. If people would open up a little more about who they are, and truly show what they are like, they might be more apt to build better relationships with those around them. Activities such as staff retreats, unannounced lunches, sharing your home for a meal, movie nights, informal book clubs, inviting speakers to the office, or simply random shutdowns of the office foster a more open environment. I love and enjoy walking our family dog with my players. Just me, the player, and our dog—conversation definitely flows differently. One of the things we try to do as a team is to build up those relationships between the coaches and players—and among the players themselves—so that we can establish bonds that bring everybody together.

Of course, this is an area in which I know we can always do a better job, whether it is through eating dinners, having more ropes courses, or anything outside of basketball, to develop the team further. The most important aspect of relationships is time. Coaches must take the time to get to know their players—where people come from, what their values are, and so forth. This is why I use the "Choice Not Chance" mantra to guide my thinking as a coach. I always make a conscious effort to mix this approach with the "person/situation" understanding, which I explained in Chapter 10, while creating an environment of honesty and integrity. You have to let people know who you are and where you come from; this will help them understand why you think the way you do. In turn, you must assess the *situation* when analyzing someone's actions and/or remarks and fight the desire to take things personally and/or out of context.

Additionally, there is an enormous element of *care* in coaching. You have to learn about the players and staff on and off the court, and organize team-building events. It's also important for a coach to share his or her vulnerabilities at an appropriate time, and to understand how your personal choices affect the way you spend your time. You have to realize that your choices, although they may seem insignificant occasionally, *do matter*. Sharing your choices and the consequences of those choices helps all in the group register a sense of your "self."

There's no job on earth where you can simply create a checklist and mark off boxes as you accomplish the tasks. You must integrate your belief system and values into the work you do. I know how important it is to share my world with my players; however, I also have to be careful about how often I discuss Maddie or Jack. I blend this as best as I can, and sometimes it is a delicate balance.

It all takes time; there's no question about it. Yet I've learned that the more a team has genuine questions about the boss's or leader's life outside of the practice floor or office, the more likely they are to be on board for the right reasons—and the more their leader can do the same.

REFUSING TO GIVE UP, NO MATTER THE OPPONENT

One fact that I know to be true about basketball (and pretty much all sports) is that nothing makes you as eager to get back on the court again as losing a game. All you want is to get rid of that "just lost" feeling. That was our attitude going into the game against Notre Dame, even though we knew it was going to be a difficult challenge.

We got off to a good start and had a 13-point lead early in the second half. That quickly evaporated, however, when Notre Dame went on a 17-point run. The Irish led by six (66 to 60), with 59 seconds to play. Even though the Irish fans were already leaving the building, our kids were not ready to give up.

Incredibly, Lindsay Bowen was fouled on a three-point attempt and made all three free throws. She then made a three-pointer, with 14 seconds left, to tie game at 70. Notre Dame missed a shot at the buzzer and the game went to overtime.

Lindsay scored five more points in the extra session, and we played great defense and came away with an 82 to 73 win, one that we would reflect on many more times that season. Being six points down with less than a minute to play is a tough obstacle to overcome. However, having to do it against such a great opponent on their floor—in front of fans who were already confident of their success—*really* pumped up our confidence.

Three weeks later we went to Hartford to play defending national champion UConn, a very tough opponent anywhere, but especially at home. Coming into the game, UConn was 201 and 5 at home over the previous 11 years, and we played in front of the school's thirty-first consecutive sellout of more than 16,000 fans.

Although the situation was clearly intimidating, I believed our kids were ready, and sure enough, they went out and played a great game. Lindsay was again our leader, scoring 21 points. We won 67 to 51, really quieting the crowd. It was UConn's worst loss at home in 12 years.

I was so proud of our kids, who had ice in their veins and a calm composure. One of the challenges a coach faces when a team is playing really well and has a special moment like that is to let them enjoy it without getting too carried away. It's a challenge to refocus their attention and snap them back to reality before you have to play again.

Luckily for us, our next opponent was Michigan during the first game of the Big Ten season—and nothing gets someone from Michigan State's attention faster than a game against the Wolverines. The team's veteran players also helped capture our attention; they knew we had enjoyed success in the nonconference part of our previous couple of seasons, only to run into some rough spots in the conference games. It was critical for us to get off to a good start in the conference—something the players realized and made clear to each other.

Though we beat Michigan by 10 points, we didn't play well and lost at Ohio State (which was ranked ninth in the country at the time). That was when something seemed to click for our team—when they became aware that they really did not like to lose. That put us on a roll during which we won 16 of our next 17 games, losing only at Penn State.

One of the best moments of the year came when we beat Ohio State, which at the time was ranked number two in the country, at home before a crowd of more than 14,000 people, the largest ever to watch a women's game at Michigan State. The environment was electric, and the crowd went home happy when Kristin Haynie hit a foul-line jumper as the clock ran down. Ohio State missed a shot at the buzzer, and the fans stormed the court after the win—an incredible event for our kids. A win against Michigan during our next game allowed us to tie for the regular season conference title; we then went on to win the postseason tournament championship.

One of the most gratifying parts of our success for me was looking up in the stands at home games and seeing more than 6,000 people at our games. It was almost three times the number of fans the women's team was drawing when I got to East Lansing. People were beginning to recognize our players when they walked around on campus. Not only were our team members buying into our program, but the fact that so many fans were turning out as well made it clear the future was very bright indeed.

The only thing that worried me at that time was how we would perform in the NCAA Tournament. I had talked about championships since getting to town, and I think the players realized now that was not just a dream. We actually had the type of team that could make a deep run in the NCAA Tournament. Yet I also knew from experience that a large part of success in the tournament is dictated not only by luck but by the luck of the draw, including our matchups against particular teams.

We received the number one seed in the Midwest Regional. It came as somewhat of a surprise, since Stanford, which had been ranked number one in the latest poll before the selections, actually came out as number two. Yet we were a legitimate number one seed by RPI measures. It was pretty remarkable that we had beaten Notre Dame and UConn on the road. I wanted the chance to play them again, primarily because it would mean we finally had advanced past the second round and made it to the Sweet 16 and Elite 8.

We almost didn't get there, which is where the element of luck comes into play. After beating Alcorn State in the opener, we faced USC in the second-round game. We won, but only because Rene Haynes picked up the ball off the floor in a true scrum and managed to put it in the basket amid the chaos, thereby clinching our 61 to 59 win.

We played like the number one seed meant something, as though our rank would win the game for us. We were a little bit affected with a slight fan mentality, something against which I always preached. We played like we were supposed to win the game just by showing up. I was incredibly upset that we exuded such an attitude, and I was furious as I made my way into the locker room after the game. I cursed up a storm as I challenged the team to play *our* way—no seed entitlement attached. No fear allowed, either, since we'd missed shots for fear of losing rather than attacking dangerously as we had done all year.

"This is not how we think! I don't recognize you and I'm not going to coach you," I fumed. We were in the Sweet 16, and even though that was where we wanted to be, it wasn't good enough. Our focus and mind-set were so off that I had to find a way to remind the girls that we were better than that—because we were.

I think that game served as a wake-up call, which is something we all need in our lives every once in a while. We won our next game against Vanderbilt by 12 points, setting up the game against Stanford. I knew it would be close, and it was.

We had just over one minute to play, and were ahead by five points. I told our team during a time-out to play a man-to-man defense to change up the pace; however, we really couldn't defend Stanford in a man-to-man because they were quicker than us. Freshman guard Candice Wiggins got the ball, scored, and was fouled. She made the free throw, which put us ahead by two points instead of five, with 50 seconds left.

Everything happened so fast. I called another time-out and confessed to the team that it was my mistake. It was a coaching error, I said, and pointed to myself. "You guys are great," I said. "That's on me." I called a play and Lindsay hit a jumper for her only basket of the night. We exchanged baskets, and then Lindsay hit two free throws in the final seconds for the final margin of victory.

That win meant a trip to the Final Four. Governor Jennifer Granholm came into the locker room and she talked to our team after the game. It was the first time for me that any governor was a part of our postgame celebration. It was such an incredible honor to have a woman of such power, grace, and intelligence addressing the team. What's more is that the men's team won its regional and was headed to the Final Four as well. It was a happy time around East Lansing; however, I didn't want our girls to feel satisfied, because we still had work to do. There was no time to celebrate; we had to focus. Preparing for a Final Four is truly a great balancing act, and we were eager to get it right.

Our national semifinal opponent was Tennessee, coached by Pat Summitt, who had been in this position many times before in her illustrious career. She certainly had the edge on me in terms of experience, but I could not wait for that game. I had been to the Final Four before on two occasions, as Joe Ciampi's assistant at Auburn, and I certainly was familiar with Pat and her coaching style from all of the years I spent in the SEC. Two of our assistant coaches also had Tennessee ties; one had worked on Pat's staff for seven years and another had played for her. It felt perfectly natural to me for us to be playing Tennessee. It also was a fun matchup because Al Brown had been a coach at Tennessee and now was in his first year with me at MSU.

The Final Four was in Indianapolis, which was where we had won the Big Ten championship. It was also close enough for our fans to be able to travel and enjoy the experience. Ironically, the men's Final Four was in Saint Louis, just a four-hour drive away; I knew a lot of people who were planning on taking in the men's game on Saturday, then driving over for our game on Sunday.

The men lost to North Carolina in the semifinal game, and our fans did not want to be disappointed two days in a row. Fortunately for them, we played a truly amazing game. Tennessee was leading by 16 points with seven minutes to go, and I think most of the crowd had already decided that they had clinched the National Championship. But our players simply refused to give up.

We started chipping away at the lead, and finally, with 58 seconds left in the game, Kristin Haynie stole a pass and went in for a layup, giving us a 64 to 62 lead. After the Volunteers tied the game, Kelli Roehrig's basket put us back in front. Tennessee missed three chances to tie the score, and after we got the rebound on the final miss, Victoria Lucas-Perry scored, to give us a 68 to 64 victory.

I was so proud and happy for our players; however, I was not surprised. They had not quit on me or themselves all year, and there was no way I expected them to quit when they fell behind during this all-important game. The win was exhilarating—truly an out-of-body experience the likes of which I have never experienced before or since. Watching Victoria streaking down that floor with the ball, knowing she was going to secure the victory, was a moment I will never forget. There was no point in that game that I was thinking of the outcome until I could look at the clock and see that there was no time left.

I will never forget looking across the court and seeing our athletic director, Ron Mason, crying. That was how much this game meant to everybody involved. Coming back from 16 points down in a national semifinal game against Tennessee with seven minutes remaining was certainly worth a tear or two, as far as I was concerned.

Not all of our fans were at the game, of course. Many more were watching on television, including John's father, T. Hook McCallie, who was 93 years old and living in a nursing home in Chattanooga, Tennessee. I found out a month or so later from his nurse that he was terrifically excited watching us play. I recalled him telling me earlier in his life, "You are going to have to beat her [Pat Summitt], you know." And he watched on television as we did.

His nurse informed me that he had gotten sick soon after the game and never regained his health sufficiently to watch the National Championship game. John's father actually thought we had won the National Championship when we beat Tennessee; he didn't know there was another game to play. The last thing he saw in his lifetime was us beating Tennessee and Pat Summitt, as he had instructed me to do years earlier. He died about two months later.

Unfortunately, we still had another game to play; this one was against Baylor, a team that had made it to the finals for the first time by beating Louisiana State. While playing for the national title was obviously incredibly exciting, we had played the late game on Sunday night—and having to prepare so quickly for the finals was yet another learning experience. It wasn't something we'd done before, which was all part of the process. Tom Izzo and head football coach John L. Smith made the trip for our game, which was a sign of tremendous respect for our program. We went on to play Baylor in the National Championship game and, although we came up short, learned many valuable lessons.

There was no denying how far we had come in five years at Michigan State. I knew the administration was happy, and they rewarded me accordingly with a new contract. I was so confident in the school and what we were doing that I didn't really bother to read it. I threw it in a drawer in my desk and went back to work.

I was not going to be satisfied with finishing second, and I didn't want our players to be, either.

Throughout the year, Coach P has team meals at her house as a way for the team to connect and enjoy time together away from basketball and school; she's shown here with the 2009–2010 team at her home in Durham, North Carolina.
Source: Personal Collection

CHAPTER 12 QUESTIONS

- Do you invest in your team by spending time with them away from the office?
- Perseverance and battling adversity make success possible in all circumstances. Can your team fight back from behind and rally to finish?
- Is your team consistently authentic?
- Do you take risks as a leader?
- When you make a mistake in your personal or professional life, do you own up to it?
- Has your team ever been in "the zone" (i.e., so focused that they could not be denied)?

A MESSAGE FROM COACH SMITH AND COACH WOODEN

WINNING ISN'T ALWAYS ABOUT WHO HAS THE BEST OR MOST TALENTED PLAYERS

What caught me a little by surprise in the summer after our loss to Baylor was the reaction our team received from a lot of people I never expected had been paying any attention to us.

On a Nike trip to Whistler, British Columbia, I found myself suddenly drawn into a conversation with legendary North Carolina coach Dean Smith. I had never met Coach Smith before and didn't know he was going to be on the trip. He was accompanied by a bunch of other people from his state, and he suddenly walked over and began talking to me.

"I really like your team," he told me. "Don't tell anybody, you guys were my favorite women's team this year."

I was still upset and felt bad about losing the championship game, and I started talking to Coach Smith about his career. He said, "If I can remember correctly, the first time we went to the Final Four we lost the first game."

I looked at him and smiled, and then he said, "That makes you ahead of me." His gracious remarks simply overwhelmed me at that moment. Coach Smith was such a gentleman, and I couldn't help it when a tear started to run down my face. His claim that I was ahead of him was the biggest joke I had ever heard.

Another incredible event took place that same summer, when I received a package in the mail. It was a children's book from iconic UCLA coach John Wooden. I had no idea why he had sent it, but he included a note that read, "Congratulations on a great season. I really liked your team."

I also got a letter in the mail from San Antonio Spurs head coach Gregg Poppovich conveying the same message—how much he liked our team. I found the recognition from these legendary individuals fascinating, and was so appreciative of those gracious words from some of the truly amazing folks who have helped define the sport.

I could completely understand why everybody liked our team: The players were total winners and total fighters. I think both Coach

Smith and Coach Wooden appreciated the smart and clever way in which we played. There were no all-Americans on that team, not even any who had earned the title in high school, but they worked hard and played very well together.

The lesson I took away from that team and that season was that winning isn't always about who has the best or most talented players; it's about which team plays the best. That is true in any team sport, and it is true in the business world as well, because that's really what a company is: a team of workers, all trying to achieve one goal—an organization's success. It takes a combination of people, all doing different tasks, but working together to achieve that goal.

We had fallen just short of achieving that, but still had come such a long way and accomplished so much that I couldn't have been prouder. I also knew that our success had come as the result of nothing but good old-fashioned hard work, which, as far as I'm concerned, is the only real way to live. The key to flourishing in any line of work is to surround yourself with people who can make you better. Being around productive people—those who want to learn, live, and chase dreams—can inspire anyone to do more and do better. Folks with a great spirit who bring the same enthusiastic energy every day to all they do naturally make others want to improve themselves as well.

Effective leaders lead by example, inciting a mind-set in their team members that nobody will work harder or be more productive. Different people work at different speeds; some can get more done in an hour of work than others can, but that doesn't mean that one person is less productive than another. A good leader is one who takes those different people and different habits and blends them into a cohesive unit. A leader is someone who teaches a philosophy, acts with consistency and reliability, and understands a given situation and person on a daily basis while driving his or her team to achieve their personal and professional goals.

People often misunderstand leaders because they don't have all of the information, even though they often think they do. My team members think that what they see in the office is all that happens in my world, and it takes time for me to explain that this isn't the case. There have been occasions when members of my staff don't understand a decision

I make, because they don't know half of what I do or where I am getting my information. However, I am the one who is held accountable. Effective leaders have to be able to withdraw, seek advice, and evolve.

A good leader will acknowledge when it's time to remove him- or herself from distractions in order to think, strategize, plan, and make decisions with care. This often requires soliciting guidance from someone in your position—or preferably higher. You need to look upward, asking "Who has been in my seat?" Those are the people to whom you should gravitate for decision-making guidelines, thinking, and advice.

I don't think I have ever forgotten that my foremost responsibility as a coach is to the players on my team. When I recruit a player who agrees to come to my school, I am basically telling her parents that I will be responsible for her. These mothers and fathers entrust their daughters to my care and guidance; sometimes that means sending their children (who may never have been away from home) clear across the country, to a different environment, with different friends, to a totally different experience. That is a major commitment, and one that I never take lightly.

Watching those players develop and grow as young ladies is rewarding to me. I want these women to leave my program as better people—and better basketball players—than when they came in. I want to send them out into the real world ready to lead productive lives and be valuable citizens. I get a real kick out of staying in touch with my former players and hearing when something great happens in their lives.

I received a rather amazing e-mail one day a few years after the loss to Baylor—not from one of my former players, but from a Baylor player. The following e-mail was a reminder of the rewards one can reap from coaching and teaching:

> I know this may seem random, but my name is Chelsea Whitaker and I was the point guard for Baylor when we played against your team at Michigan State. I have been meaning to write you for the longest time and I just never got around to doing it.
>
> I was just letting you know how awesome I think you are as a person and coach. I remember when all four of the Final Four teams were sitting in a room trying on our [tournament] rings. I was sitting by myself absorbing the experience when you sat down beside me, introduced yourself, and [began a] conversation [with me]. We started

talking about . . . how awesome it was to be there. [While] I know that seems simple, I'm sure you know better than me how some coaches put themselves on pedestals and detach [themselves] from other people.

I have secretly admired you ever since our encounter that day. It was so refreshing to me to see someone with your pedigree just sit down next to me and have a normal conversation. I remember thinking to myself that I could have played for this lady any day.

I was just writing to let you know how I felt about such a subtle gesture you made to me and how happy for you I am that you got the job at Duke. I wish you success throughout the rest of your career.

It was signed, "God Bless, Chelsea."

Talk about making my day. The e-mail from Chelsea might have been narrow in regard to coaching; however, it was widely relative to the lessons I've learned, and how those lessons can be applied to other walks of life. It was the kind of message that leaves a coach energized and secure in the knowledge that he or she can make—and indeed, has made—a difference in somebody's life.

COMING CLOSE CREATES ADDED MOTIVATION

Coming so close to winning the National Championship gave the entire team the motivation we needed heading into the 2005–2006 season. We also knew, of course, that all of our opponents would be ready for us and that there was no chance that we could sneak up on anybody this time. One comment I repeatedly make to all of my teams is to be "all about us," and it definitely applied in this situation. We were not concerned with who we played but rather how we played—while continuing to "think right" and attack together.

Coming back to beat Tennessee did teach us a valuable lesson, one I think we never forgot. For whatever reason, my teams seem to make a habit of making inspiring comebacks. They were all examples of how we learned to stay in the moment as a team and remain focused on our *next play*, which is something we discuss all the time. It is a philosophy I learned from reading Coach K's books, beginning in 1993. That term has become a part of me ever since I really began to study, follow, and admire Coach K. The notion of the "next play" truly frees teams to stay in the moment, because everyone must understand it and commit to focus.

We reached the Sweet 16 and a matchup against Duke when our magic ran out; the Blue Devils simply had too much height and too much depth for us. Though there would not be a repeat trip to the Final Four, I don't think any of our players felt bad about the season. I know our seniors could look back on outstanding careers, and I came away from both the game and the season proud of and thankful for how hard they had worked.

One personal reward for our team's success came when I was chosen to coach the 2006 USA FIBA America's Under 20 team in an international competition in Mexico City that summer. It was there that I received another lesson about what's really important in life.

For some reason, I had left my wallet in the bag that I took with me to the gym for our games instead of leaving it in the hotel safe. I had warned our players and staff that we were in a foreign country and that they should be extra cautious about our belongings.

We had a great tournament and won the gold medal. We were a dominating team that broke many USA records. I went to look in my wallet for something while everybody was celebrating. When I couldn't see it, I thought somebody had stolen it during the game. Our bags were behind the bench, and fans were sitting right behind the bags, so it was not a great leap to assume that it had been taken. Everybody was in the middle of a big celebration, and I was going crazy because I thought my wallet and passport had been stolen. My first thought was as a parent: "I can't go home tomorrow." It was an instance in which emotion trumped reason almost entirely. John was with me, and the kids were back home. I tried to smile for the team pictures, but my mind was totally preoccupied.

Nobody else knew what was wrong; finally, I told Carol Callan, who was in charge of all of the women's activities for USA Basketball, that I could not find my wallet. Carol replied, "Okay," seemingly without getting overly concerned. I walked outside, when another thought hit me: All of my baby pictures of Maddie and Jack were in my wallet. I started crying, because I knew that there was no way I could ever replace those photos. At some point, Carol calmly asked me, "Joanne, do you think you could have put it away?"

I answered that I would check, but that I didn't think so. Everybody else went to the restaurant for a celebratory dinner, but I hightailed it to my room—where I found my wallet. I didn't want to admit to anybody that I had found my wallet, since I had made such a big deal about it being missing. Finally, I quietly and sheepishly went over to Carol and told her I had found it. I could get back to celebrating again with the team.

I was trying to be a coach, a wife, and a mother simultaneously; because of that, I really couldn't join the celebration and lose myself in the joy of winning the gold medal. My mom has always pleaded with me, "Joanne, could you just try to not work so hard all the time." I thought of that statement almost immediately after I found my wallet. I am grateful to be a coach, mom, and wife (baby pictures and all), but it isn't always easy trying to be all three, especially at one time.

I told Maddie the story later and said that losing those pictures really would have been something worth crying over. Everything else in the wallet could have been replaced. It was a lesson to me about what was really important in life versus what was really *not* all that important—and how balancing these can be so difficult.

Thinking about all of those childhood photos left me in a reflective mood. I had been at Michigan State for six years, and I was proud of our record. Yet despite our success, I could not escape the feeling that something did not seem quite right, that something was missing in my life.

Counting the four years I had played at Northwestern, I had completed 10 years in the Big Ten. I had enjoyed a lot of great moments, but a lot of scary ones as well, such as the night our plane almost went down during a snowstorm in Iowa. For the first time, doubts began to creep into my head about how long I should stay at Michigan State. My life with John and the kids was a dream come true, but I couldn't help but wonder whether there was a better life waiting for us somewhere else—one with more challenges and a better quality of life relative to travel, weather, and longevity.

Following the passing of North Carolina State women's basketball coach Kay Yow after her courageous battle with cancer, Coach P was interviewed to discuss Kay's impact.
Source: Duke Photography

CHAPTER 13 QUESTIONS

- What kind of impact does your team make, regionally and nationally?

- Are you open to feedback in your professional and personal life? Can feedback empower others?

- Does your team stay "in the moment"? Are they ready for "next" right away?

- Throughout your life, do you have moments of complete overload? How do you respond and recover?

14

COACH K TEACHES, "DO WHAT YOU CAME HERE TO DO"

Moving On

We were preparing to play in the 2007 NCAA Tournament when I got a phone message one day. One of our administrators was clearly frustrated by the fact that I had been talking with the athletic director at another school about a coaching job. "Well, Joanne," I heard on the message. "If you think you are going anywhere, just check that contract and the buyout for $475,000. We own you."

I replayed the message until it truly sunk in. I was stunned. What was she talking about? What did that mean? What buyout?

With shaking hands, I quickly opened my desk drawer and pulled out the contract I had signed (without really reading) after the 2005 Final Four. I was shaking, I was so nervous. I flipped through the 12-page document, almost hyperventilating. I finally saw the number . . . $475,000. She was right. "Oh my God," I said out loud. I couldn't believe it.

I raced home to John and showed it to him. I told him we were stuck, that there was no way we could get out of this deal. After a while, we both decided we had to do something to figure out what options we might have.

I went to see athletic director Ron Mason, but got nowhere. That was my buyout, he said, and he was not going to change it. I couldn't believe everybody was *this* serious. I could quit, but that was not a legitimate option. I would still have to pay the buyout before I could coach anywhere else. I was really deflated.

My players, of course, had no idea any of this was going on, which was the one thing that made me happy. We had played very well in the tournament opener against Delaware and won by 11 points. Our next game was against Rutgers, a very good team that had beaten us by six points earlier in the year.

Rutgers was more athletic and more talented in many spots; we fought valiantly, but to no avail. They won by 13 points, and I was not surprised that they got all the way to the National Championship game before they lost.

It was over, and I knew it. I will never forget looking up into the crowd at the Breslin Center one last time. I was sad and despondent as I gave a sheepish smile and wave to the fans who had supported us so fiercely over the years. I could not cry; I was numb. I had no feelings left. The fans knew I had been considering another job and that I might be leaving, but they had no idea what else was going on.

Michigan State had me in a bind, and they knew it. I tried to talk to them about changing the buyout clause, but the school wouldn't budge. They offered a slight salary increase in my rollover contract, but the amount was still less than what some other women's coaches were making in the Big Ten. Worst of all, they gave me an ultimatum: I either had to sign the contract or I was gone.

I saw no real alternative and agreed to sign the contract. However, I made certain everyone knew I was doing it under duress. What had been a great relationship suddenly was very cold and bitter; memories from 2005 had long since evaporated.

We also had to plan the annual team banquet we have at the end of each season while all of this was under way. The banquet is really for the team, especially the seniors, and I didn't want my personal situation to detract from what should be a memorable night for them.

I was probably the only one who was squirming in her seat that night when University president Lou Anna Simon appeared in a taped video message. She made the usual remarks congratulating the team for a great season, then turned her attention toward me and essentially stated how glad she was that I was going to be the coach there for the rest of my life.

Of course, this overwhelmed me completely. I was too young to have made that kind of commitment, yet I knew I was stuck. I had to sit there and listen and try to smile while I thought about the trap I was in. If I wanted to coach, I didn't see how I could do it anywhere but at Michigan State. There was nothing real about it, and I knew I was in trouble.

The clear lesson for me, and for others, is to read and understand your contract (or any important document) thoroughly before you sign it. I'm not embarrassed to say that I completely trusted the people at Michigan State. I felt very good about my surroundings and about the people who surrounded me. Life often gives you new things to learn and new people to meet, and I think one of my strengths is the wonderful naïveté I have about life. I tend to think that things will always work out for the best if everybody acts reasonably. Unfortunately, this scenario was testing that outlook.

Contracts are meant for those special times when circumstances can become unreasonable, when emotion can come into play, distort reality, and make life miserable for both parties. As somebody who once aspired to be a lawyer, I know how important contracts are and how important it is to ask the questions in advance, because one can never predict the future.

This was all extremely difficult for me because, while I did have a contract at Michigan State and was thrilled to work there, I felt that the wins we had over the years should have permitted removal (or at least reduction) of the buyout. It was a matter of principle; however, it was their choice. As we become more successful in life, it's only natural to seek increased freedom and latitude from our employers. Unfortunately, that just was not happening in this situation.

The issue was not just with the contract, as far as I was concerned. It had more to do with the fact that I had truly moved the women's basketball program at Michigan State in a new direction during my seven years there. We had set a new precedent, yet I was not being recognized in an appropriate manner.

My only releases during this stressful time were John, the kids, our great neighbors, and my players. I tried to pour all of my attention into those areas so I wouldn't think about anything else. I decided that, for my well-being, there were certain individuals at Michigan State with whom I would no longer talk, because there truly was nothing I could say to them. Lou Anna called me to tell me that I had to try to reengage with some folks, and she tried again to use her iron-fist approach. I just told her I couldn't do it. An eerie numbness had started to take over my actions.

Then, out of nowhere, came the phone call from Duke. Even under the best of circumstances, I would have been very interested in that job; however, I was in a particularly unique situation. It took a few days to get everything resolved, including the buyout, but it was finally accomplished. We were going to Duke. Sometimes in life, you just have to go through the process to learn. This contractual negotiation was a new thing to me, especially at this level. I was not an expert at the time. Leaving a great place like Michigan State for an even more challenging top-ten program like Duke's seemed to require growing pains.

We knew the announcement was going to come out the following day, perhaps before then, knowing the media. When I called Ron Mason and told him I was resigning to take the Duke job, he was very honest and kind to me. He told me I needed to call two other administrators and the president so they would not hear about it on the news.

I woke up Lou Anna and told her I wanted to thank her for everything she had done for me, and that I had accepted the job at Duke. She was very nice and wished me well.

The news came out the next day, and I was quoted as saying that Duke was my "dream job." It made all of the headlines, and I wish I had never said it—because, of course, the writers misquoted me, and people from Michigan State took offense. I loved the state and the people, but that didn't come across in the media's treatment of my decision.

I was immediately treated like dirt. The school shut off my cell phone and took away my car, leaving me without a way to get home. I started to clean out my office and was told I had to be out in a ridiculously short amount of time or they would be kicking me out. I packed furiously. My assistants didn't know what to do because they didn't know if they would be going with me, staying, or looking for a job somewhere else. I had to confirm the news to the team, and I cried when I did it. Though some of them did, too, some were really pissed off. It was a short meeting, because once you say you are leaving, there really isn't much else to say. I told them that I knew they might never understand it, but it was the correct decision for me at that time.

I made appointments to go see Lou Anna and Tom Izzo, because I felt as though it was the right thing to do. Lou Anna was all ready to take notes, and I told her I was only going to say great things about my time at Michigan State. Perhaps out of support and graciousness, she wore a Duke blue suit. I learned a lot from her, and grew up a lot because of her. Having competed against her many times on the golf course, all in a friendly way, I finally concluded that this situation was like a golf game to her—one that she was trying to win. She was very gracious in our last meeting, and I left thinking I had just defeated her on the golf course.

The meeting with Tom was far different. I wanted to thank him for all he had done for me and for how graciously he had treated me and my family. He was as cold as I had ever seen him. He simply asked, "Why?" and then looked away from me.

I tried to explain to him how I was tired of the Big Ten after 11 years combined as a player and coach. I explained that we wanted to be closer to John's family and that I thought I would get the new challenge I needed at Duke. I got up to give him a hug as I left, and he gave me a very aggressive couple of pats on the back. It was a chilly departure.

I knew I would see Tom again one day, and I wondered how that meeting would go. It actually did not occur until shortly before the start of the 2010–2011 season, when both of our teams were playing in the Jimmy V Classic, and we both came to a pretournament banquet in New York.

There was a big cocktail party before the dinner, which I attended with my sister Carolyn because John was not able to come. Our director of athletics, Dr. Kevin White, Jacki Silar, and all of the Duke folks were there, with a total of about 400 boosters and supporters in the crowd. They made an announcement during the middle of the party that they needed all of the head coaches there to gather in the back of the room for a photo. As I walked to the back, I thought to myself, "This is going to be funny."

Sure enough while I was standing there waiting for the photo, somebody came up behind me and grabbed me in a big bear hug. It was Tom, and he kind of kissed me on the cheek from the back. I jokingly told him he was mean for saying what he had said in the newspapers [regarding my departure from Michigan State]. He said smiling, "I wasn't mean, I just had to toe the company line," to which I replied, "You *are* the company line." It was a relief to have such nice back-and-forth banter that was friendly and warm, but honest, too.

Soon, everyone sat down at their own tables for dinner. ESPN's Mike Tirico was the emcee, and all of the coaches were expected to speak for a few minutes. There were two women's team coaches there, myself and Gary Blair of Texas A&M, and four men's coaches. As the only female, I was asked to speak first.

Tirico was asking me questions, when all of a sudden, out of nowhere, came a question for which I was *not* prepared. "So, Joanne," he said, "What's it like to be part of a Tom Izzo program and a Mike Krzyzewski program?" I paused for a minute, and the crowd grew silent, because everybody there knew my history with Michigan State. I told him how incredible it was, and then added, "To tell you the truth, I was kind of hoping to coach the men's team at Michigan State," which drew a big laugh from the crowd. "Tom said no, so I left."

Tirico then said, "Well, Mike's not going to let you coach the men's team at Duke, either," and I said no, I didn't think so. That brought laughs from the crowd, and it was a relaxing exchange, fun and therapeutic.

Tom started talking about me when he came up to speak later in the program, which surprised the heck out of me. He said how nice it was to see me again, how much he had enjoyed it when I was at Michigan State, and how amazed he was by what I had done at Duke. He added, "It's hard to have somebody leave, and she left us." It was a poignant moment, and it really amazed me. He didn't have to say all that, but I really appreciated it. I was completely touched and moved, and it became an incredibly healing moment.

I had always known that I had an authentic relationship with Tom, one that had been built on my huge respect for him. He had the National Championship, and I wanted what he had. Any genuine connection in the business world has to be built on a response to values. Thus, the people with whom you choose to connect reflects your response to their values. You have to search inside yourself and ask, "Who do I want to be around?" It had been very purposeful for me; I wanted to be around Tom Izzo in much the same way I wanted to be around Joe Ciampi. Too many professional people tend to forget about that philosophy.

After the dinner, Carolyn and I bumped into Tirico in the hotel elevator. I accused him of trying to set me up on purpose (albeit in a good-natured way), and he said to me, "Joanne, you don't remember, do you?" and I just looked at him with a blank stare. "Remember what?"

"I'm from Ann Arbor," he replied. "I watched your 2005 team closer than anybody, along with you and Tom. I just had to stir it up a little bit." It was a perfect ending to a night that was all about human action and healing, and none of it had been planned. It just came about because people were willing to let it happen. Tom reached out and didn't avoid me, and I joked with him and Mike Tirico. The occasion left me with a lot of energy, and the feeling that a tremendous weight had been lifted from my shoulders.

The lesson in this story is evident: People have to work through issues and not quit when faced with conflict or difficulty. When trying to find a way to heal, it's vital to remember that humor is truly one of the best healers. A leader who has the ability to be a bit self-deprecating can allow others to move forward. It's very different than saying, "This is my way and this is the way it's going to be." The three of us involved in this situation had the ability to kid about ourselves, which led to some powerful healing.

MEETING ANOTHER CHALLENGE

Saying yes to Duke left me with another tough decision to make. I had been selected to coach the 2007 USA U21 Women's National Team as it competed for the FIBA World Championship in Moscow in the summer of 2007, an experience I was very much looking forward to. However, coaching that team would force me to make a time commitment that would pretty much take me out of recruiting and training for the month of July, a key period for the success of any college team.

I received great support from Duke officials to continue coaching the USA team. The ultimate challenge was in front of me, but maintaining my commitment to USA Basketball had come first. I did not want to let the folks at USA Basketball down because of the trust they had placed in me, but my loyalty was now to Duke as well. This once again left John in a position of having to sell our house in East Lansing and handle all of the packing and moving while I was out of the country. It was another sign of how much I trusted that John could do this— and do it well—without my help. I knew that the decisions I entrusted him to make were in good hands.

Unlike our move from Maine to Michigan State, I had something new to worry about: the effect it would have on our children, particularly Maddie, who was 13 at the time. That is a difficult age for a child to move and abandon her friends; unfortunately, there really was no alternative. I knew she was hurting, so I worked it out with USA Basketball that she could come on the trip to Moscow and stay by my side the whole time.

Interestingly, Maddie and I did not talk about the situation and the move to Duke very much. I didn't want to force her if she wasn't ready, and I knew there would be a time and place when it would come up.

The trip was amazing. We played the Russians in the semifinals on their home floor; I can remember 8,000 Russians in the stands ringing cowbells. We dominated the Russians, then went on to play and beat Australia for the championship. It was a great feeling to win another gold medal in an international competition.

Getting to Work at Duke

I was excited to get to Duke and get to work. The university was a place where I felt a connection in one way or another since they had first started recruiting me as a high school sophomore. I think I somehow just knew I would wind up there one day, and that day had finally arrived.

One of the most exciting opportunities to me about coaching at Duke was getting the chance to work near Coach K. I had read all of his books and considered him a major influence on me as a coach, even though I had never met him before I came to Durham for my job interview. Because I felt as though I knew him just by reading his books, I was excited to think about how working this closely to him could make me a better coach. I was excited about the possibility of learning from him, the same way I had learned by watching and talking with Tom Izzo.

Another coach for whom I had tremendous admiration was Kay Yow at North Carolina State. Although I did not have a personal relationship with her, I could tell she was a great teacher, mentor, and all-around person. When I showed up at my first ACC meeting, Kay was sitting down with an open chair next to her; she saw me, tapped the seat, and said with a big smile, "I think you need to sit right here."

We sat and discussed a variety of topics, and I began to develop immediate respect for her. We talked about Duke, and transition, difficulties, and faith, and everything else you can imagine in a very short period of time. Kay died of cancer not long after that, but in the short time I got to be with her, she made a very large impact on me and my life. I am amazed about her impact still today, even though she is no longer with us physically.

The job seemed from the outside as if it would be absolutely perfect; so I was surprised early on about the mixed signals I was receiving as I settled into it. I was locked in a naive world, trying to see only the good and not the bad. One of the people with whom I had discussed my position from the very beginning was Lonny Rosen.

I knew there would be a period of transition with the players, who did not want to see their former coach resign. I had to decide whether to rehire some of the assistants and staff or let them go, and I was determined not to penalize people who did not deserve it just because their coach had left. I wanted to be thoughtful and reasonable in my decisions. I was thrilled that Bobby Sorrell and Lauren Rice, who already were at Duke, accepted my offers to become part of my staff. I also brought a couple of my former assistants at Michigan State with me. New coaches have to be patient when hiring assistants and other staff, and not judge some of the candidates who are already associated with the program.

I know a lot of coaches who just clean everybody out when they take over a program; while that might seem like the easiest and simplest way to do it, I don't think it's the best way. I valued the work that Bobby and Lauren had done at Duke, and knew they could continue to make a positive contribution to our program.

I have been a head coach for 20 years. I've had two assistant coaches move on during that time, and both of them found special things. One went on to become a head coach, and the other went back to her hometown. Though it can be difficult, a leader who sees that a change is necessary must have the courage to handle the situation and help the people they're leading find something for which they are better suited. Employees themselves often won't even recognize the situation. It's hard, but it benefits them in the long run to hear that they need a change of venue and a new mentor.

Many people take the attitude, "Well, I contributed, so I deserve to be here." Their sense of entitlement is staggering. I don't have perpetuity or job security as a head coach, so my assistants don't have it, either. I want everybody on my staff to work at the job as though they are going to be a head coach someday—because I want them to be. Good assistants have that philosophy, and they also have great energy.

My assistant, Al Brown, has been with me for eight years now, starting during my time at Michigan State. People are always interested to know what my connection is to Al, and it's really pretty simple: I don't want to be the oldest member of my staff. With his silver hair and cool sweaters, Al is like a father figure for our team. He brings a maturity level that our team and staff need, not to mention the fact that he is a very accomplished and savvy coach. Our long-term relationship has grown out of mutual respect and an appreciation for trying to offer our team the very best in teaching, player development, and overall improvement. Maturity and intelligence are probably the biggest advantages in helping a team advance. I have spent a lot of time teaching that to my younger staff. Al is clearly a mature adult figure, and his presence creates a very different dynamic with the team.

Part of an assistant's job is to understand the big picture. I like it when my assistants aren't afraid to make suggestions and bring up new ideas; however, the approach they use matters. If someone says to me, "Coach, I know you like to do X and I see why, but do you think there's any way that Y would also fit it?" That's an assistant who recognizes philosophy, who gets it. Some assistants will make random suggestions without using reason or understanding the fundamental philosophy. These are the kind of suggestions that are the most difficult to incorporate.

Young assistants (and employees of any kind) need to realize that what they do is a craft. You have to learn your head coach (or manager) inside and out, and study all the facts about him or her. Assistants in any field must show sweat equity, where they are willing to put in the time and passion as if they were the head coach. They must make it clear that they want to consider and pursue being a head coach. They must learn and listen while demonstrating an incredible work ethic.

With change, you have a choice, and it can be inspiring or depressing. It's a personal choice that everyone involved must make. I knew I was dealing with a lot of hurt people as we went through the transition phase at Duke. It really affected my ability to coach, because the basic message I was receiving from the players was "Just coach us; don't change us, and don't ask anything about us." This was really hard for me as a coach who really wants to get to know her players and treat them like extended members of her family. When I invited the players over to my house for dinner, it seemed like it was an imposition for them, because it wasn't something they'd done before. Each coach has his or her own philosophy and style, and I worried about what I was going to do if the players were not going to be receptive to mine.

An especially tricky part of the transition was that these were obviously talented players who had done very well so far in their careers at Duke. They were also intelligent young ladies, which led them to question why I was trying to do things differently than had been done before. And I couldn't really blame them for asking this.

Lifting weights was probably the first battleground. I had learned over the years, especially at Michigan State, how important it was for me to get the players working with weights to become physically stronger. A tougher player gets more rebounds, holds onto the ball better, makes a better team member overall.

Every day of that first season was an adventure and a lesson in working with change. These women needed to talk and have somebody listen to their concerns; however, that couldn't be me—at least not yet. I was not in a position at that point where they felt they knew me or could trust me. As a result, I was not able to provide what these kids needed and wanted. Of course, that left me feeling very frustrated and wanting time to pass more quickly so that I would no longer be the new coach.

Our early-season schedule did not help matters much, either. We had an incredibly challenging schedule and lost three games in a row. It was uncharacteristic at Duke, but understandable given the arduous schedule, the transition, and the fact that we had no returning all-American players on the team. I was left questioning many things that had always seemed second nature to me. I loved coaching, and I thought I was good at it. But during that time, I was unsure, sad, and wondering what was next.

COACH K GIVES ME THE MESSAGE
I NEED WHEN I NEED IT

The next game on our schedule was at home against Rutgers, which happened to be ranked fourth in the country in one poll and third in the other. I was alone in my office with the door shut; I didn't want to see anyone. Though everyone needs alone time occasionally, this was something else. I was trying to close myself off from the world.

I was questioning my decision to come to Duke, and I was a physical and emotional wreck. I couldn't even do what came most naturally to me: prepare for the next game. I was at my lowest point and felt completely isolated.

Suddenly, there was a loud knock on my door. I didn't want to see anyone and didn't know who could be knocking like that; usually, one of my assistants let me know if somebody wanted to see me. I didn't even look up; I kept staring at my desk and said under my breath, "Come in."

Coach K walked in and shut the door. I looked at him and our eyes clinched. No words were spoken—but everything was said. He knew everything that was troubling me, and I knew he knew.

"How are you doing?"

I just shook my head. I didn't cry, but I was only able to muster, in a low monotone, "It's not what I thought. It's not what you said." For years I had read his books and believed them, fantasized about coaching from his experiences, and imagined the world of basketball the way he created it—and it was not that way at all. I felt as though he had portrayed an image of something that wasn't real; this was not what he had made Duke seem like, not what I had come to believe or expect. It seemed to me at that moment that he was the person most responsible for my misery; yet he was the only one trying to help me through it.

He started talking. "You are going to learn something quick here," he said. "You will learn that these people have nothing to do with you. Do you understand me?"

He kept talking, telling me stories of when he first came to Duke, how people were having trouble accepting this new Polish guy and how they were all over him. "Screw them, screw all of them," he said, referencing any folks who could not understand this transitional time. He repeated it more emphatically. He was aware of things I didn't think he would have paid any attention to, and he was telling *me* not to pay attention to them. "What [other people] say doesn't matter," he said. "They have nothing to do with you—or your team."

I can't recall all that was said that day. The fact was that Coach K had come to me in the middle of the day, in the middle of the season. He had a thousand other things to take care of, but he showed up to care for me at my lowest moment. The essence of his message was "Do what you came here to do." He emphasized why I was there and reminded me that nothing else mattered.

He knew that our next game was against Rutgers. He wished me luck in the game and let me know that even if he was not watching, he would be listening. Then he left my office. I looked at my clock—he had been there for an hour and a half.

It was a cathartic moment, an emotional cleansing that stripped away all the bad feelings. No one could ever know what Mike did for me that day. I went back to work preparing to play Rutgers with an entirely different attitude than I had felt a couple of hours earlier. Coach K had provided me with the exact message I had needed at the exact moment I needed to hear it. It was a locker room pep talk like no other. The motivated fighter in me was suddenly back—the coach who loved challenges and wasn't going to let criticism and doubters get her down.

MY FIRST BIG WIN AT DUKE

When the Rutgers game started, we were all of a sudden down 9 to 0. I called a time-out and really got on the team. God only knows what they got from me. I told them in no uncertain terms what we were and were not doing, and somehow, it just clicked. We came back and won the game.

It was funny how many people magically showed up to congratulate me after the game. Their entire attitude was "Thank God, Duke did not lose four in a row." I didn't give a flip about that sentiment.

The one person I wanted to talk to after the game, other than my family, was Coach K. I finally found him the next day and told him he had just won his first women's game at Duke. He smiled and put his arm around me; he told me that we were both primed to move on to play better and that more victorious games were ahead for both of us.

I think the most crucial lesson I learned during that first season at Duke was how to handle adversity when people haven't placed much trust in you. Those players didn't know me, so they didn't trust me. It is easy to have faith when everything is going well, but what happens when life gets a little more difficult? Your faith had better grow by leaps and bounds when the situation gets tough. It really is the only way you can overcome those obstacles. My initial difficulty at Duke was a humbling experience; looking back, I think I could have done better. But I can only learn from what happens and move forward.

I realize now that there was no magical way for me to get those players to trust me. I had to earn that trust, and the only way to do that is by acting consistently over time. I also had to experience my own learning curve.

I don't think I really understood the level of passion, either love or hate, that Duke sports inspires before I walked on to the campus. It hit me quite hard, however, when I went to make some public speeches. Usually you have an audience that appreciates you, but I spoke to some groups that seemed to be 100 percent North Carolina fans. At times like that, I wondered why I was asked to come at all! I quickly learned there were a lot of people in the state who hated Duke and viewed it as the school up on the hill that appeared unreachable. I was used to Michigan, where the fan base was split about fifty-fifty between Michigan and Michigan State; however, that wasn't the case in North Carolina, and having to get used to that was a huge adjustment.

I also learned that year how coaching and leadership are personal, which is never more apparent than when things are *not* going well. Everybody is on your side during the good times, but how many people are still standing there beside you when things *aren't* going so well? That's when you have to have the confidence and internal drive to keep doing what you are doing, because *you* know it is right.

We did manage to get through that first season one way or another, and statistically it was not all that bad. We won two games in the

NCAA Tournament before we lost in the Sweet 16 round and finished the year with a 25 and 10 record. Neither I nor the players were pleased with that breakdown, but I was not going to measure our progress that season simply by the team's record.

TRANSITION AT WORK AND AT HOME

I knew I was developing a process, a chemistry, and a philosophy at Duke, as I had done at Maine and Michigan State. The Duke team had enjoyed more success in recent years than had the other schools where I coached, which made the job and the transition more difficult. After all, why would I make changes if the team was winning?

The only way I could answer that question was to respond simply: I was doing the things the only way I knew how to do them, the way I had done them before and the way that had made me a successful coach. I was excited to share my philosophy, but just as eager to learn more. I was also making changes by blending the old and new together. I wanted to grow as a coach and get better.

The Athletic Coast Conference (ACC), in which Duke played, provided a different level of competition than the Big Ten or America East Conference had. We began running more multiple defenses, and our team became more athletic. I wanted to capitalize on our players' strengths, one of which was their intelligence. Any leader has to have confidence in his or her own ability to lead and make tough decisions and must be able to stand the heat and criticism if those decisions prove to be unpopular.

I was more concerned about the transition that my family was making that season than what was happening with the team. John got a job teaching in Chapel Hill, North Carolina and was fine. Jack was still too young to really have many memories of Michigan, and he was adjusting well. The person with whom I was most concerned was Maddie, and she was having a tough time.

Maddie was attending the Durham Academy, a wonderful, private smaller school. She had not been going there very long when she came to John and me and told us she wanted to go Riverside High School, a public school, starting with the ninth grade. We asked her to tell us why, and her answer mainly had to do with the fact Durham Academy was small and did not offer enough diversity. She also wanted to play basketball and volleyball for a larger (and, in all likelihood, more competitive) school.

Maddie had a long list of reasons, and she obviously had thought long and hard about this decision. We asked her if she was sure that this was what she wanted and she said yes, so we agreed. We did not want to squash Maddie's enthusiasm, and letting her pick where she wanted to go to high school was definitely a positive step and a huge sign that she was maturing quite a bit.

A lot of parents tend to underestimate their kids; however, if you can let yourself trust them, especially as they get older, they develop a greater sense of power and confidence. It is, of course, undoubtedly difficult—and much easier said than done. But parents, like bosses, have to recognize opportunities when they come up and empower their children to make decisions regarding those opportunities. Our decision to let Maddie choose her school was the right thing to do— for a lot of reasons. The headmaster at Durham Academy asked me what they had done wrong, and I told him, absolutely nothing. Though it was clearly a great school, it was not right for Maddie at that time in her life, given the enormous changes she had just undergone.

I was thrilled to be able to do something that made my kids happy; it gave me more energy and determination to try to find more happiness in *my* job as well. I also was excited because Duke had hired a new athletic director, Dr. Kevin White.

I was stunned that Duke was able to lure Kevin away from Notre Dame to take over for Joe Alleva, who had gone on to Louisiana State University. Kevin had been the athletic director at Maine earlier in his career, but had left just six months before I was hired. All I heard at Maine was how great Kevin was; he had left behind a pack of incredibly loyal supporters.

Kevin actually came back to teach a class in sports management at Maine during the summer while I was there. I audited the class just to find out why everybody kept saying so many great things about him. I wanted to learn as much as I could about the great Kevin White and see for myself why everyone in Maine thought so highly of him. I knew he was somebody I could learn from.

Kevin knew I was the women's basketball coach; but other than that, he didn't know me at all. I told him why I had taken the class. I know I asked a lot of questions; I was constantly trying to find out more about him and how his mind worked. As I've emphasized before, I always try to pay attention to mentors and to people who do their craft incredibly well. As an aspiring coach, I wanted to learn from the very best.

One thing I did know was how much the people who had worked with, and for, Kevin in the past admired and respected him. It was obvious as soon as he arrived on campus in Durham that he knew what he was doing and knew what was important. He brought a new and fresh image to the job. He took the time to listen to my experiences and concerns. I could tell the athletic program was going to take off in an exciting direction with him in charge.

Kevin was very positive; he assured me that everything was going to be great and that we were going to make a fresh start and work together to get things done. It was just like the pep talk I received from Mike before the Rutgers game: exactly the motivational speech I needed to hear at that particular moment. No athletic director had ever spoken to me so candidly. Kevin somehow managed to strike a balance between being businesslike and personal. His focus and passion quickly made me a believer.

I was still kind of recovering from what he had said, when he looked me directly in the eye and said, "How about we go out to football practice?"

I just laughed, but out we went, into the misting rain, to watch Coach Cutcliffe and the team. Standing there getting soaked, I was the happiest I'd felt since arriving at Duke. Though it had been hard to come back from vacation, I was now excited and ready to go.

However, I still had one piece of unfinished business. I'd put off taking the test for my North Carolina driver's license because I knew it would mean having to give up my Michigan license, my last official tie to that state.

I cruised through the sign portion and started out okay on the written exam; then the questions started getting harder. Of course, I had not studied the book. I had been driving forever, so how could I not pass this test? I missed six of the 20 questions; since you can only miss five, I flunked the test.

I was sobbing and furious with myself as I got back to the car. Luckily the windows were rolled up and nobody could hear me. I don't ever remember losing it like that, even during all the pressures of our move, Maddie's adjustment, learning to navigate Duke, and so forth, yet all of it had been symbolically expressed in that botched driver's exam. Amazing how displaced emotion can surface at the oddest times. I finally collected myself enough to call John and tell him what happened.

He actually started laughing when I told him, which finally relaxed me. It became a good joke for our family, and a happy memory, especially after I went back and passed the test a week later. And this time, I didn't think I was too good to study.

Just as my life was looking up again, however, another shock sent me reeling.

Coach P sharing a laugh with Coach Mike Krzyzewski prior to "Primetime," a program for Duke University employees to create a dialogue with officials on campus, at the Bryan University Center on the campus. Coach P spoke briefly about building a team and was followed by Coach K, who spoke about his experience building the USA Basketball National Team from 2006 through winning the gold medal at the 2008 Olympics in Beijing, China.
Source: Duke Photography

CHAPTER 14 QUESTIONS

- Whenever you enter any agreement or contract, do you read it thoroughly and understand all the terms?
- Do you understand all contractual language?
- Can you separate "situation" from "person" in difficult times?
- Do you know how to properly thank people?
- Do you forgive and learn after difficult times? Do you apologize and grow?
- We all seek the truth. Can you handle the truth when someone gives it to you directly?
- Are you able to keep faith and build trust when you find yourself in a new environment?
- Do your colleagues admire your work?
- Details matter. Are you organized enough to allow them to work for you?

You Have to Seek Out the Changes—and See How You Need to React to Them—to Make the Team (and Your World) Better

I was back in Maine on vacation in August 2008 when both my mother and sister mentioned that they had noticed a change in a spot on my forehead as they watched one of our games on television. It was a little circle that I had always joked was my birthmark. But my family members weren't joking; they begged me to get it checked out by a doctor when I got back to Duke.

I delayed the visit for a while, but finally went. As soon as the doctor examined me, he said, "We need to get that off right away."

I thought he was kidding about the "right away" statement, but he was serious: He wanted me to undergo surgery the next day. After Dr. Zen cut out the mole (a most uncomfortable process), I thought everything was going to be okay. Yet the longer he looked at it, I could tell something wasn't right.

When I asked the doctor what was wrong, he said he couldn't say, that they had to wait for the lab tests. When he called me back (after what felt like years), he let me know that he hadn't been able to get all of it, and then gave me the frightening news without mincing words that it was a malignant growth—melanoma. He told me that he would have to operate again and that I might have to undergo chemotherapy, because they were worried about the nodes.

They wasted no time performing the second surgery. Though they eliminated all of the cancer this time, it left an ugly scar on my forehead. It was yet another experience that made me realize, and redirect my attention to, what really was important in my life.

While I was sitting at home with a big ice bag on my forehead, the telephone rang. It was Coach K. It was a busy weekend for him and he had a lot of recruits in town, but he let me know that he had found out about my surgery and was concerned (I had not told him about it). He asked if I needed anything and wanted to know what he could do to help. He was incredibly caring and supportive. That phone call from him was all I needed to begin feeling better.

When I went back to work and saw Coach K, he took one look at me and remarked, "Wow, they got you pretty good." He was the only one who looked right at me, confidently, in a way that no one else seemed able to do. I had stitches across my forehead, and kind of thought I resembled Frankenstein. I appeared that way for at least a month. I will never forget the way that Mike just really *looked* at me. Most people turned away, and very few people actually asked me what was wrong.

It was a scary time, but luckily the doctors' quick work prevented what could have become a much more serious problem. I do still have to get all of the moles on my body checked every six months— something I do without hesitation to make sure that I stay healthy.

I had a difficult time, though, when people started calling me a "cancer survivor." The term *survivor* indicates to me that you have *endured* something; my entire experience with cancer was over so quickly that I didn't really think I had suffered very much. I did think about how much Coach K had helped me through everything; and that got me thinking about former North Carolina State men's basketball coach, Jim Valvano, who died in 1993 after a yearlong battle with cancer, and also about Kay Yow. To me, Kay was an ultimate cancer survivor. Her battle was long term, and she battled so bravely and courageously that she was a true inspiration for so many people.

The tremendous respect I have for Coach K stems very much from the friendship he had with Valvano (who went by the famous nickname "Jimmy V" throughout his career). Mike went and visited Jimmy V every day in the hospital before he died. It isn't just his success as a coach that makes me admire Coach K; it's that, in addition to fighting for his team, he was a fighter for so many others—a fighter beyond measure. And his reassurances to me in those tough times helped rekindle that fighter instinct inside me as well.

I needed this spark reignited at that time more than ever, because I was reminded nearly every day that I needed to keep that attitude if I were to be successful and overcome all of the obstacles we faced as we settled into life and coaching at Duke. Luckily, I was also able to talk about these issues as they surfaced with men like Coach K and Lonny Rosen. My conversations with them continued to lift my spirits, as they assured me that things would get better. I believed in these people, so I listened to them, and I just knew their advice would almost always be right.

I was asked to do a Nike clinic with two of the best men's coaches in the game: North Carolina's Roy Williams and Syracuse's Jim Boeheim. The honor I felt to be included with these two excited me, as did a conversation I had later with Roy during the clinic. He had left a very successful Kansas program to come back home to coach North Carolina, and he was able to win a National Championship in his second year. I saw Roy as somewhat of a kindred spirit; we were working under similar circumstances in dealing with change. We had both chosen to transition to incredible positions at historical college powerhouses in the triangle after succeeding in programs we had cultivated ourselves—and to which we had brought national attention.

I was determined to use all of the knowledge I had gained during my first year at Duke to my full advantage in the second year. I was interested first and foremost in my relationships with the players. I knew we would all have to undergo a transition period; they were missing their old coach during this time and wondering why they had to learn my way of coaching. However, my first year—and the related adjustment phase—was now over. I felt more ready to communicate with the players and encourage them to do the same with me. I was aware of, and thrilled about, the fact that I was now coaching very smart and driven kids who chose to be at Duke and to pursue the highest standards, both on and off the court.

I came to see very quickly how my Duke players operate at a different level of thinking than many college kids. Their grades matter to them; they consider their academic work to be an important element in their overall happiness. I knew I needed to work with them on having balance in their lives and to try to dissuade them from constantly seeking perfection. That can be a very dangerous chase, since a focus on process always beats the pursuit of perfection.

I also tend to bristle at the idea that players are either yours or somebody else's. I didn't feel as though I had inherited these girls from a previous coach; after a year, I simply felt that they knew each other, they knew me, and I knew them. I wanted to be their coach, lead them, take on the difficult issues with them, and learn and grow from them. I knew that building relationships was something that we'd continue over time; it would never be something that we "finished." It was a time of growth for all of us.

I can recall one interesting conversation I had with a player once about the role of a coach. This young lady told me that she thought of a strength coach as a strength coach, and a pastor as a pastor. But because I was her coach, she didn't really know how to categorize me. She liked to put everything in a little box, give it a label, and never venture outside of the definitions she had selected.

What she wanted from me as her coach was to tell her where to go and what screen to set—and she would be fine. I laughed when she told me that, and said I couldn't do it, "Because I'm not a robot," I explained. "So I can't coach like a robot." I could sense that it was easier for this player to try to compartmentalize everything like that. I also knew that this tendency was limiting her ability to express herself on the floor, not to mention affecting her overall productivity. And I told her so.

I also told her that I thought she was putting those kinds of labels on everybody because she had endured a tough family situation and wanted to box everyone in. She looked at me strangely, then paused—for a long time. But I continued, "If you box us in and keep us in our separate places, we'll never get too close; and if we never get too close, you'll never lose anybody again." She just sat there as I told her, "I'm not going to be boxed in."

Sometimes you cannot meet your players' expectations, and a lot of the time, that's a good thing. It allows you both to grow from the conversation, while teaching each other about individual boundaries.

I wanted to put myself out there for this kid—to share my authenticity with her, show her that I was real, and express my concern for her life beyond what she accomplished on the basketball court. Even if the other person is skeptical and unsure, building relationships sometimes requires going out on a limb like this.

The way I deal with players has changed as I have gotten older, gained experience, and as my own children have grown. I have been able to use what my children and others have taught me in my interactions with players: It is important to break out of that little box. We can never say, "Let's do it like we did last year," because no two years and no two teams are the same. It is critical to seek out the changes, and determine how you need to react to them, to improve both yourself and your team.

In my opinion, any good coach could be just as successful in other business leadership roles. The most important skill a coach has to have to lead a team well is the ability to communicate with, inspire, and teach his or her players. The same is true in the professional world. I found my way into coaching by accident; yet the longer I have been at it, the more I believe it was what I was born to do: inspire, teach, and empower. And, yes, sometimes it requires conflict. It's not all roses, and adversity certainly clarifies.

The knowledge that I had gained that first year, and the renewed motivation I felt going into year two, left me with the belief that there was no way we could *not* succeed. I was cultivating the process on a daily basis. A coach has to take that pressure off of the players, remove the high expectations, and let them concentrate on staying in the moment and keeping the game *fun*. The process becomes fun only when people are enjoying it, which serves as all the motivation they need.

Many of these players had developed a protective wall around themselves emotionally; they were trying to keep everybody, including me, out. I made it my goal to proclaim that this was going to be the year we broke through that wall; we were going to grow and improve together.

I cannot claim that I treat every player the same, because I don't. No coach can make that declaration if he or she is being honest. Though I love all of the players the same, I favor the ones who work the hardest; I won't apologize for that. That speaks to a level of productivity. I can't help but admire the kids who have gotten the message I constantly try to send: that the harder they work, the more productive they'll be—and the better they will feel about themselves. And the reward will be increased playing time, as well as stronger, more mature relationships between us and among the other members of the team.

It seems to me that many people nowadays have forgotten the importance of working hard and relishing the effects of hard work. The idea that you can get something for free, or that you are somehow *entitled* to something, is the most bizarre notion in the world to me. I believe in the individual pursuit of happiness and that a crucial element of being happy comes as a result of experiencing a day of hard work.

How much fun do you think the season would be if coaches had to give every player the same amount of time, no matter what? Chances are, it would be the most uninspiring, ridiculous situation ever. Regulating competition in such a way sends a poor message to people. On the other hand, inspiring a competitive cauldron and supporting the players as they compete fosters incredible productivity and creativity in everyone. Fighting for an opportunity and learning your role—and how to maximize it—is a fundamental life lesson.

If I have a senior player who is working 500 times harder than somebody else, there's no way anyone can tell me I have to play her the same as another kid. It's certainly okay (and necessary) for young folks to learn early that you must compete, challenge yourself, and then eventually accept your role on the team.

One of the beauties of athletics is that sports can teach the valuable psychological lesson that every player, and every person, truly has the ability to rise to his or her own highest level. Though that level will differ for every player, the coach who can elicit each person's maximum talent—and compel her to perform the best she can—will be very successful in the long term.

I also will not apologize for the fact that I treat seniors differently than others and give them a lot of leeway. I won't deny it; I will go to the ends of the earth for my seniors. Freshmen get to make their share of mistakes, but they won't get the same treatment as the seniors. They have to understand that's how I operate, because I feel that they must earn their stripes. Commitment, longevity, and loyalty are important elements in any team.

I do not, however, believe in having a doghouse mentality. Everybody makes mistakes, and you have to grow from there. I did take this approach a bit more as a younger coach, because I viewed myself as "traditional and tough." But I learned over the years how limiting that was. I don't want to have an adversarial relationship with my players unless I need to temporarily do so in order to stimulate their development. Basketball is truly a game of mistakes, on and off the court, and teaching from those mistakes is critical.

Coaches must give players guidelines and make the consequences for their actions clear. If a certain situation causes me to react angrily, I want the player to know it's because she has not done what I asked her to do. If a player asks me why she is not playing, I will respond, "Do you think it's because you have not done X, Y, or Z?" Coaches generally don't forget, especially in context to the whole.

I also think the players know what is going on most of the time, and they know it just as well as the coach. They become very easily distracted by a nonperformer. I can have 11 people giving me a terrific effort in practice, but if just one is not working to their full potential, there comes a point at which the players want to check that person, too. In that situation, I usually have to approach the disruptive player individually and say, "I want you to work in the weight room tomorrow instead of coming to practice." Then we will see how the next practice goes. The same is true in the business world. Nonperformers can be a distraction. Leaders and managers must have a plan for those who clearly are not productive and therefore compromising the whole.

Players (and employees and, really, anybody) simply want to feel good about themselves. They want to feel as though they are playing to the best of their ability, and they want to be rewarded for their hard work and performance. Though we usually measure success in sports in terms of wins and losses, that's not the only way to do so. However, since it's how the media and fans decide who is the "best," that outlook occasionally trickles down to the players, even if they understand that what matters isn't as simple as a game's outcome. A good leader drives the team right back to "process" and allows the results to come naturally.

Measuring success that way would indicate that we got off to a strong start in the 2008–2009 season. We won 17 of our first 18 games, including wins over Stanford, Oklahoma State, and Maryland—all ranked among the top 15 teams in the country.

You never know when, where, or who a compliment is going to come from, and I was reminded of that when I got on an elevator one day at Duke and ran smack into Bobby Knight and his wife. He was at Duke visiting Coach K but I hadn't known he was there.

He said, "Hey, Coach, good to see you." As I began to introduce myself, he said, "I know who you are. I like your team. It's good to see you." Though I had never met the man before in my life, he then went on to tell me, "I like good basketball, and I like your team."

We *were* a good team; he was right about that. We ended up 11 and 3 in the ACC, good for third place, and then lost to fourth-ranked Maryland in overtime in the postseason tournament. I knew we were going to get a bid to the NCAA Tournament; but there was no way I was prepared for what the committee chose to do.

They sent us to the first- and second-round site at East Lansing, home of Michigan State. I was stunned. I knew the only reason for it was to try to create some buzz over a Duke–Michigan State matchup on television, with Coach P returning to coach against many of the players she had coached as Spartans—and for those student-athletes to have a chance to play against me and my new team.

I was embarrassed and angered that my personal situation would be used in this way. The NCAA Tournament should be nothing more than a fun opportunity to find out how good you can be and a reward for a great season. The team is always extremely excited, and March truly is the best month of the year for them. Unfortunately, the NCAA's decision had focused the entire story on me. It was awkward for me, and what's even worse, it took away any possibility that our team would have a festive environment. It affected my former players, too (although they did enjoy the last laugh).

We beat Austin Peay in the opening game, setting up the game ESPN wanted: Duke against Michigan State. It didn't go well. Michigan State had the advantage of playing at home, even though we were the higher seed. The arena was energized, and everybody enjoyed cheering against me and the Duke women. There was no way our players should have been exposed to that kind of environment or treated that way. It wasn't fair and it wasn't right. Though home court advantage for a lower seed is a reality in women's basketball, personal revenge, so close to my departure from MSU, was just too much. Not enough time had passed to remove the additional motivation.

That game should never have been about me. It should have been about the Duke players against the Michigan State players; yet that was merely, and regrettably, a subplot. Our players were in no way prepared, nor could they have been prepared, for the booing and screaming and yelling that was directed at me. It was yet another difficult lesson for all, as well as a distraction our players did not deserve. My history with Michigan State should have had nothing to do with the game. Michigan State played its best game of the season and really came ready to play.

The worst moment of all was when we got on the plane to fly home. My family had, of course, been at the games, and Maddie was the most visibly upset by what had happened. She was crying because those fans had been so negative toward her mother. I think that might have been the moment when Maddie truly said good-bye to East Lansing and Michigan State.

Having had a personal experience with Duke Cancer Center, Coach P was the keynote speaker at the first Duke Medicine Regional Cancer Summit in the spring of 2010.
Source: Duke Photography

CHAPTER 15 QUESTIONS

- What kind of adversity have you faced throughout your life? How has it made you better in business? With your family?
- Do you compartmentalize your relationships? Do you create open relationships to learn multiple lessons from an individual?
- What do you do to ensure that the "process" is your process?
- How do you handle nonperformers?
- How do you deal with events that are outside of your control?

RECRUITING IS A TRUE TEST OF WILL, DISCIPLINE, CHARACTER, AND EVALUATION ABILITY

GETTING THE RIGHT GROUP OF PLAYERS

I was heading from Oregon to Atlanta and on to Orlando. It must have been July, the height of recruiting season, and my least favorite time of the year.

Recruiting is a true test of will, discipline, and character, yet it is also the most vital component of building a winning team, no matter what the sport or gender. A coach can know all of the X's and O's and be the best motivator around, but if she doesn't have the right group of players, all of the coaching in the world is not going to turn them into a championship team.

One of the realities of coaching at Duke is that recruiting is much more thorough than it was at Maine or even Michigan State. Because Duke is at a different place academically, we have to recruit players on a national and even international basis. We have to find girls who are a fit for the school and then determine as well if they are a fit for our team. Though it's a challenging process, the fact that our academic standards are able to draw student-athletes from all over the world creates a great sense of pride.

The only way to honestly evaluate players is to watch them in person and try to talk to them and their families so you can get to know them. Even though it was one of the greatest experiences of my life, the two summers I spent coaching with USA Basketball did hurt me a bit on the recruiting trail. I did not get that time to see and meet some players whom we might have been able to recruit.

The level of recruiting has been very challenging as well, because we are competing against the top schools in the country for the very best high school players. I believe we have narrowed the gap on those schools, thanks to being able to sign and bring on board some of the highest-quality players. However, you can never rest, because other coaches and schools are not resting, either. They're constantly going after the "next" special player.

One recruiting reality I never had to face before I came to Duke (and therefore one for which I was not prepared) was the feeling of absolute love or hate that Duke seems to provoke in people. There really isn't any middle ground; people are either on one side of the fence or the other.

Duke's standards incite that wonderful animosity that allows us to stand out as a unique academic and athletic opportunity for young people.

Spending some time in the business world, particularly in sales, helped prepare me a little for what recruiting is like. You have to be able to foresee people's hesitations, share your passion for what you sell (in my case, Duke) openly, and enjoy overcoming any objections to choosing a school with standards like ours. Everybody loves to attack success, and I am much better now at dealing with that than when I was 28 years old.

One interesting criticism that really surprised me seems to occasionally come from people within the state of North Carolina. Our campus is a mere eight miles from the University of North Carolina, and there are not many people who are fans of both teams. It has even been used against me that my husband, John, teaches at North Carolina, as if that is some kind of incredible negative. The academic world continues to collaborate among all institutions in the triangle area. However, the athletic world stands alone and remains competitive beyond measure. Most people recognize the enormous collaboration that takes place on the academic side between the schools around here; however, the rivalries on the courts and on the fields are an entirely different story!

One of the most difficult parts of recruiting is the loneliness. I don't know how many times I have been alone in a quiet hotel room late at night, really missing John and the kids. I get this big pit in my stomach that churns right through me and sometimes emerges in the form of tears. I say "I am so sorry" out loud, over and over again; I know I am talking about my kids and the quality time I am missing with them that I am never going to get back. But one good therapeutic cry usually gets me through the recruiting period. It is amazing how there can be clarity in tears.

Any job requires an employee to make some sacrifices; there is always give-and-take, good and bad. There are a lot of wonderful things that come from my profession, and I love what I do. The need to balance and reenergize is always tricky.

One of the biggest problems with recruiting during July is that the kids are spread out all across the country; they play too many games; they forget that winning can be fun; and they get too tired and worn out.

I am a natural recruiter; I enjoy making the calls and the entire process. I love it when potential students want the best of both worlds (academic and athletic) that Duke has to offer at the highest level. Duke is not for everyone, but all of the coaches are very proud when we find young people who are the right fit and decide to come to school in Durham.

I also feel an incredible sense of responsibility when I am recruiting a 17- or 18-year-old player; I am essentially promising her parents that I will be responsible for her for the next four (very important) years of her life. Deciding where to go to college is a major decision for any youngster and his or her parents, with so many variables involved; I have already seen evidence of how difficult it is within my own family.

When we were back in Maine for vacation, one parent asked me if he should be concerned about college and scholarships for his daughter, a basketball player, who was not yet a freshman in high school.

I told him, "You should be concerned about her health, her confidence, her balance." He told me his daughter's high school coach was worried about what her fit would be on a collegiate team. I was absolutely astonished; she had not yet spent even one day in high school!

My reaction must have been obvious, because this parent finally looked at me and said, "I'm getting carried away, aren't I?" It just reminded me that even the things we think are most obvious aren't always so to others. These parents get to experience the recruiting process only a couple of times—perhaps only one time—in their lives. I have to remember that these folks are not out living in the recruiting world every year, as I am. Perspective is so important.

Parts of the recruiting process that I really enjoy are going into a prospect's home and then having her visit our campus, which is when we get to show her what Duke is all about. The campus visits pull the recruiting all together for the prospect, the team, and the staff. The home visits help me see what kind of a player and person I am getting. I can tell a lot about someone's background by visiting her home. I can see the way she was raised and what her parents and other family members are like. This really gives me a fairly complete picture of who these people are. No two people come from the same background, and it is really educational to see all of the different environments in which young people have been raised. Some of the obstacles that their families have had to overcome are incredible.

I have also seen the flip side of this—instances in which people who have everything they could possibly want don't realize how great they have it and just take everything for granted. This sense of entitlement generally starts at home. But the bottom line is that we try to assess a player's passion, drive, and hunger to compete, regardless of the environment in which she was raised.

Recruiting is the ultimate balancing act between my duties and responsibilities as a mom, a wife, and a coach. I know other women deal with this quagmire every day; it is very challenging, and it changes daily. And, although July is always a tough month, some other months are extremely rewarding and enjoyable. One of these is in June, when we have our summer camps for high school and grade school kids.

I am constantly amazed by how many coaches tell me they don't like these camps. Some of them don't even attend, even though they carry the coach's name and parents are paying lots of money to send their kids to that particular coach's camp. I love our camps and would not even dream of not being there the entire time (unless I have to recruit).

Dating back to my years at Maine, I have always involved our players in the camps. I use this as an opportunity for the players to be together and learn some of the business responsibilities in running the camps. Instead of bringing in outside coaches, I have our players run the camps. The seniors have more responsibilities than the younger kids, but even the younger ones work up to those leadership roles. We pay the kids for their work within the guidelines set up by the NCAA.

The kids who run the camp realize how much organization and preparation is involved and how hard they have to work for the process to be successful and productive. It is a real bonding experience for the team, not to mention a lot of fun.

Though my players are used to this by now, that wasn't always the case. When I first started this tradition at Maine, and then in the first years at Michigan State, and even at Duke, the players couldn't understand what I was trying to teach them by having them run the camps. They couldn't see how the experience could be translated into what it would be like if they were running their own small business—not to mention the chemistry created by time well spent as a team. Yet gradually they learned what I am trying to accomplish, and this past summer, all the players really stepped up and made camp special. Camp is the only time my current players and I are teaching together and it really makes that a time special for me. The cards of thanks and warm words and testimonies come to our office long after camps are over.

Of course, we still have issues that we have to overcome; some players don't understand why someone might make more money than they do, for instance. Though it's usually due to the fact that certain individuals have more experience or are performing a different task, they don't see it that way. It's a life lesson about developing character, and every time you teach character it becomes contagious to the team. Productivity and experience drive the paycheck, which is a pretty vital lesson to impart to young people.

I knew we had made progress and were getting closer to where I thought the program could be, should be, and was expected to be by the start of our third season (2009–2010). My third season at both Maine and Michigan State had been our breakthrough year, so I was not surprised when this team played well and had a similar kind of season. One of the highlights for me was going back to play at the University of Maine, which thankfully was a far different experience than going back to Michigan State had been the previous year.

The stakes were different, of course, since it was a regular season game that took place early in the year. However, the trip was still very meaningful to me. It was fun to see and talk with many old friends, some of whom I had not seen since we had left Orono nine years earlier. Taking the team out to enjoy lobster with their bare hands might have been the trip's highlight.

I could not have asked for my team to play more competitively than they did. It showed through the regular season, and we tied Florida State for the league championship; it showed when we won the ACC Tournament, as well. A tough two-point win over Maryland put us in the tournament semifinals, where we beat Georgia Tech to move into the championship game against North Carolina State. Senior standout Jasmine Thomas scored 18 points, to lead us to a 70 to 60 victory. It was a great moment for our program—the first ACC Tournament title since 2004.

One interesting fact that I learned after the victory was that I had become the first Division I women's coach to win tournament championships in four different conferences (Maine had been a member of two different conferences while I was coaching there). Jasmine was named the tournament MVP, an honor she richly deserved. We were proud of our growth and excited for more.

One of our unsung heroes in the game was senior Keturah Jackson. She scored six points, grabbed five rebounds, had two assists and two steals, and blocked a shot, playing a big role in the victory. It was a moment we shared in the postgame celebration, however, that I will always remember even more fondly.

The kids were called forward to receive their awards; Keturah made her way up to the stage when it was her turn. Instead of walking straight, however, she broke ranks and headed toward where I was standing on the side of the stage. As she got to me, she said, "Thank you, thank you," and gave me the biggest hug ever. Never could I have expected that, and it was so welcome. It was one the most rewarding, satisfying, and gratifying hugs I have ever received as a coach—because of its sincerity. I hugged her back, and we stood there for a long time.

No paycheck, no matter how big, can ever replace that kind of feeling. I called Keturah's embrace a million-dollar hug. I know she was thanking me for believing in her and giving her a chance to play. I was as happy for her as she was grateful to me. It takes an extraordinary human being to react during that kind of moment and to show and give heartfelt feelings. Everyone on that team was inspired by Keturah. She was our glue, our inspiration, and our truth; so it was incredibly symbolic that she would reach out in that way.

Our 27 and 5 season had earned us a number two seed in the NCAA Tournament, and we got to play our first two games at home, beating Hampton and LSU to advance to the Sweet 16. A victory over San Diego State gave us a spot in the Elite Eight, one win away from the Final Four. Our opponent was Baylor, a very good team that was led by an extremely talented freshman, Brittney Griner. I knew it would be a tough game; however, I also knew that it was one we could win.

The game was pretty much even the whole time; however, the officials kind of vaporized in the last minute and a half. They made some questionable calls, yet I knew I would get hit with a technical foul that would cost us the game for sure if I protested too much.

I am still haunted by the way the game ended. Our post player was hit with two foul calls that fouled her out of the game. I tried to talk to the officials, but I got nowhere.

Thinking back on it, I wish I had been more vocal and critical of some calls earlier in the game and had fought the officials a little harder. Though no one ever feels *good* after a loss, you feel worse when you don't think you lost on a level playing surface. A loss is much easier to handle if you can look back and see areas where the opponent was better than you, or at least played better. However, it's much more difficult to get over when you believe you should have won a game that was taken away from you in some way. We were four points away from the Final Four that year.

Baylor, of course, was the team that had defeated my Michigan State team in the 2005 National Championship game. That loss really motivated and drove our team for much of the following season, and I had no doubt the same thing was going to happen again this time for all at Duke.

Coach P coaching Keturah Jackson during a game at Cameron Indoor Stadium.
Source: Duke Photography

CHAPTER 16 QUESTIONS

- How do you handle recruiting for your staff and your team?
- What vision do you share with prospective employees?
- How do you use rivalries and competition to your advantage?
- As a parent, how do you motivate your child without being overbearing?

17

COMPETITIVE CAULDRON

One of the things I really believe in as a coach is the notion of a competitive cauldron. I first ran across this term in a book by highly successful North Carolina women's soccer coach Anson Dorrance. The idea is that you gather all of these kids from different backgrounds and experiences, and you're somehow supposed to mold and shape them into a team.

Though all of the players who come to a school like Duke are extremely talented, it's always interesting to see how they perform and act when they get into that competitive cauldron. Most of them had been the best player on their high school team—and now they are surrounded by players who are either just as good or better. Some of them respond to that challenge by working harder and making themselves better players. Others, however, become swallowed up by that cauldron and never become the players they should be.

Coaching requires teaching and mentoring and diving into the task at hand—being in the moment and dealing with whatever you have to deal with to make it work. Every coach in every season is going to have obstacles to overcome: injuries, players not performing up to par, and other adversities. It's always interesting to watch how different coaches handle all of these challenges: Some try to find a way to battle through the problems and still find success, while others throw up their hands and say, "All of my best players are injured—there's no way we can win." I don't think those individuals understand what coaching is all about.

Our 2010–2011 schedule was truly one of the most difficult ever assembled in Duke's women's basketball history. When you add in the fact that we were counting on getting immediate contributions from our five freshmen, the challenge was incredible. The fire and fight of this team amazed me from the moment we began practicing. They truly proved that they were capable of responding to any challenge.

The leadership exhibited by our three seniors was outstanding; it seemed like Jasmine Thomas was hitting the winning shot in game after game. It happened against Texas A&M, the eventual national champion, against Xavier, and against Kentucky. I never would have predicted it, but we won our first 20 games and were undefeated in mid-January.

Though it was an incredible feat, it was yet another experience from which to learn and improve.

Our twentieth win came at North Carolina State, after we rallied from a 22-point deficit, and was one of the most incredible comebacks I've ever seen. I love the fact that since I started at Maine way back when, my teams have all been able to come from behind to win a lot of games. The only reason I can give for that, in addition to having great players, is that we actually do work on that in practice, emphasizing time and score situations as much as possible while embracing a "no scoreboard mentality" in every game. Yet this particular comeback was about a driven team giving exceptional effort.

Unfortunately, as sweet as the victory was, that win set us up for a major fall. It was a real battle to keep the team in the process, which was understandable. It's hard to keep a group's attention (especially one with younger players) when they are succeeding so consistently. Our team had the number one recruiting class in the country, and we were 20 and 0, so I can't blame them for thinking they were doing what they were supposed to be doing. It's sometimes better to win 10 games and then lose a game as far as a coach is concerned; this situation makes the team much more likely to stay within the process and to do what needs to be done to move forward. (I even cringe a bit as I write this; I do honestly feel that if a team "stays within the process," success should take care of itself and a team can truly win it all.)

Our next game after North Carolina State was at UConn, televised on ESPN, and we got off to a terrible start and got killed. It was ugly. We came into that game with a feeling of relief that we had won at NC State, but that relief quickly turned into a potent lesson. When people are relieved, they exhale a bit; they let go and even let their guard down a little. I could tell, even in the locker room before the game, that we were not ready to play that night, nor did we understand the challenge ahead. All of us—coaches, players, and staff—felt responsible for not battling in that game. It was, yet again, something entirely new for the team—yet another challenge that compelled us to learn more about ourselves.

I tried to use that game as a teaching tool to emphasize an important concept to the girls: that you have to become a *consistently* dominating team if you want to achieve the ultimate goals. You have to create a habit of overpowering the other teams during the games that you are supposed to dominate, and that has to start in practice. I don't believe that losing is necessary in order to learn; however, it can be a vital part of the process. And teams themselves dictate that process. The UConn game gave us a lesson that we needed, and that was something that the players needed to realize. That is what we push for and what we teach. All of them had to hear that, seniors and freshmen alike.

We won the ACC regular season championship, a major accomplishment because it really should never have happened. We are the only team in the league that has to play both Maryland and North Carolina twice, since they are considered our natural rivals. This puts us at a major disadvantage, because both of those schools almost always have great teams. We then went on to win the postseason tournament for a second consecutive year, highlighted by a five-point play, which I had never seen before. Haley Peters was knocked over for a foul, just as Jasmine was hitting a three-point shot. Haley then went to the line and hit both free throws, which was the game's turning point. That one play kind of summarized what the team was like. They battled in all ways to win 32 games.

We really had a special senior class, and even though it's always tough to say good-bye to seniors, it was extra tough this year. This group chose to be "first years" with me at Duke. All four of us were eager and brand new together. We were essentially "first years" together and had spent four years as a team, even though they had signed and committed to Duke before I was hired as the coach. They might not have chosen me themselves; but we developed something special. Jasmine, Karima, and Krystal gave their hearts and souls to the program, and I was incredibly proud of them.

Cameron Indoor Stadium was packed with 9,300 people on senior night—and nobody moved after the game was over. All of the seniors talked about what playing in Cameron had meant to them, and it truly was a poignant moment. We had a brand-new locker room, funded by our great donors Jim and Susan Sabiston, our attendance was up 10 percent, and we led the ACC in attendance. It was an incredible year.

We had 14 days off after the ACC Tournament before the NCAA Tournament began. It was another new experience for our freshmen, and we made it all the way to the Elite Eight—to the regional championship game in Philadelphia. Doing so with such a young team might have been unheard of in some circles, but not at Duke. We knew we had the talent to do it, and the players did not disappoint me. It was a challenge I knew we could meet.

As far as I'm concerned, overcoming challenges is what coaching is all about. If this job were easy, everybody could do it—and compete to win a national title every year. I get such a thrill from leading a group of women who are working their tails off, who are efficient and precise in what they are doing. They practice hard and work hard because they love to compete and pursue championships every year. That's the reason they get up to lift weights at 6:00 AM. They can see and feel the energy in the gym; it's not only there during games, but while they are practicing, and that's exactly what it's all about.

Some of the best times a coach and player can share don't have anything to do with a game, maybe not even with the particular sport that connects them. I experienced one of these moments in the summer of 2010 with our star guard, Jasmine Thomas, who was about to begin her senior season and was a preseason All-America selection.

Jasmine and I were in a group of people having a discussion, and somehow we got to talking about white-water rafting, which is one of my favorite things to do in Maine. Jas looked right at me and quite simply told me she had never learned how to swim.

It was a confession that just rolled out, but I could tell that it bothered her simply by the way she said it. Jas has always been a tremendous competitor, so I was surprised she made that confession, mainly because that's something a lot of people don't want to admit, especially in front of a group of people. There's a shame factor involved, even though in a lot of cases (such as Jasmine's) the fact she never learned how to swim was just a part of growing up.

One of the sad realities in our country is that there are far too many young African-American children, boys and girls, who never have the opportunity to learn how to swim. Swimming was something I just took for granted, because I had done it all my life, but I know that isn't the case for everybody. So I was excited to help Jasmine learn how to swim and to spend some time together with her away from the gym.

Jas was nervous but okay when we got into the shallow end of the pool, where she could stand up and keep her head above the water. When I told her we had to go down to the deep end, she at first said, "I can't go there."

I told her not to limit herself, and we moved to the deep end. She held on to the side, then treaded water next to the side, where she could grab on when she needed to. After a while I looked and smiled thinking about the distance to the other side of the pool. She said, "No, no Coach P, I can't do it."

I told her I was not going to make her do anything, but that I knew she could do it based on what she had already accomplished that day. I told her there were two lifeguards watching who would help her if she got into trouble. Jas is such a fighter, and after a few moments, she looked at me and said, "I guess I have to try, don't I?" She took off and swam to the other side.

I was ecstatic. "Jas! Look what you just did!" I screamed. She waited a little while, then swam back across the pool—as usual, "pouring it on," just as she did on the court.

It was one of the most poignant moments I have ever had as a coach, and there were no fans there, no media, nobody taking pictures. To be honest, I don't even think winning a national title could make me feel the way that did. I told her she had just conquered an unnecessary fear; nothing that could happen to her on a basketball court could be more fearful that going into the deep end of that pool.

I recalled seeing a study that revealed that 69 percent of all African-American children cannot swim. I suggested to Jas as she was preparing for the WNBA and her life after Duke that this could be her cause— to go to these communities and make sure young black children learned how to swim. This was not about setting a screen or making a jump shot or the hundreds of other things Jasmine had accomplished on the basketball court. This was far more important: a life lesson that would be close to impossible to top.

I was really proud that all three of our seniors—Jasmine, Karima Christmas, and Krystal Thomas—were drafted by the WNBA. Jasmine was a first-round pick by Seattle, but ended up with Washington; Karima went to Washington in the second round, but wound up in Tulsa; and Seattle also picked Krystal in the third round before she ended up in Phoenix. One of the joys of being a coach is watching your players move on to begin their dreams, and I know playing professional basketball was something all three of these women wanted to do.

Coaching is often about challenges. Not being able to swim was a speed bump in Jasmine's life that she needed to get over. Coaches have to be able to teach kids how to overcome challenges, even challenges that have nothing to do with the sport they're coaching. And getting the chance to see that happen is tremendously rewarding.

I want to make a difference in these girls' lives. I want to have my players, and anyone else with whom I come into contact, understand what they can accomplish with patience and perseverance. What we do matters; we can help others in so many different ways.

I want my own two children, as well, to see that fighting back despite prejudice and ignorance is important. I want them to know that we are on this earth to seek the truth, to share, and to educate as much as possible.

There are so many people who need help now. They need to be encouraged and mentored, and it needs to come from the heart. Technology, with all its admittedly wonderful elements, has overtaken our world; in doing so, it has displaced the human connection we all need. Text messaging and Twitter and Facebook are all helpful in their own right, but they cannot replace the bond two people make when they are in each other's company. The new world of technology can be compulsive and destructive if we don't remember that right thinking and a sense of reasonableness matters. We need to remember the days when people actually talked to each other. Sports can teach so much, and those of us involved in mentoring are most fortunate.

I have a dream to teach and share at the highest level, to serve as a liaison to help people learn and grow and make our world a little better. I pray for strength and wisdom and the power to one day get there, dreaming big at all times.

After 20 years of marriage, John and I are still enjoying life, and we absolutely love our home and neighborhood in Durham. As we head into year five at Duke, a wonderful clarity and sense of excitement fills our home. John is a full partner in being married to a coach; I appreciate his wisdom, sense of humor, and warmth every single day. We are truly adventurers in this game of life.

What I truly want is for our children, Maddie and Jack, to be happy and healthy—always. Maddie is going off to college in the fall of 2012, on a basketball scholarship to Miami University in Oxford, Ohio. It was her choice, and we could not be more proud and supportive of her decision. Maddie told her dad that she wanted to go a place where she created the opportunity, and that is exactly what she is going to do. Miami was all her doing, and it was most enjoyable to watch her take charge of her recruiting process and "keep her power" relative to her decision.

Jack is now 12 and doing great in school. It has been fun to watch each of my children grow, knowing how others have paved the way for them and granted them wonderful opportunities.

In some ways it seems a long time ago when Maddie and I were talking to our horse, Fancy Face, back in Maine; yet in other ways, it doesn't feel that long ago at all—it seems like we are all just getting started. Maddie has made her college choice, and she is very confident and excited about going to Miami. She is ready for the next challenge in her life. I know that at 17, she is old enough and bold enough to create her own dreams, whatever they turn out to be.

John and I are very proud of our kids. As Maddie heads off to Miami, I just want to tell her to make the right choices, be in charge of her life, surround herself with good people, keep a positive attitude—and to always love her brother.

A new year is starting at Duke. A new group of freshmen are arriving from 46 states and 55 countries—a record number of applicants this year. Maya Angelou, America's most celebrated poet, will be addressing the new freshmen class, including the incoming members of the women's basketball team: Amber Henson, Ka'lia Johnson, and Elizabeth Williams.

As I sit at my desk to write the ending of this book, the trees outside are blowing dramatically, as a hurricane is hitting the coast of North Carolina. The winds are needed to end the long hot summer this far inland and bring some much-needed rain. It may wreak havoc on some of the outdoor plans, but it's also a powerful way to start a new school year. It also reminds me of our wedding day 20 years ago. John and I recently celebrated our twentieth anniversary and recalled the hurricane that hit the East coast, as far north as Maine, as our wedding ended. Roads closed, airports shut down, and the guests who had not already left were stranded. We got out cards and board games and had a wonderful time until all was clear. Instead of ruining our wedding, the hurricane actually extended it, solidifying something special.

Unexpected forces in our lives that can initially seem devastating can serve to solidify what we need, or they can bring renewal and necessary change.

I feel as though I've reached a point at which I am harvesting. Two of my former players, Candice Jackson and Joy Cheek, have joined the coaching staff. They know me, my values, and my coaching style well. As such, they bring clarity, focus, and hands-on knowledge of the "Coach P" way. After 20 years of coaching, I get to reach back and reap the seeds I've sown—the lessons I have enjoyed teaching—and can now allow my former players to teach these lessons themselves. They solidify my coaching staff and bring renewal and energy to me and the entire staff and team.

I can't help thinking about the card I happened to pull out of a deck of medicine cards while John and I were on our anniversary retreat. The card was "Squirrel," with the following kernel of wisdom:

You have gathered nuts by the score,
Exactly predicting if you'll need more.
Teach me to take no more than I need.
Trusting Great Mystery to harvest the seed.

Maddie enters her senior year of high school; Jack enters the sixth grade. They are both anticipating being on good teams, working hard, and having a great year. As I try to think about what they have been through with their mom, who is also a coach, my glance falls on a plaque I keep on my desk. It has inspired me through these last 20 years, since I started coaching and when I married, and, ironically, the words come from Maya Angelou: "I think a hero is any person really intent on making this a better place for all people."

Maya Angelou has expressed the kind of person I want to be for my family, players, and staff. It resonates with my process-driven coaching and parenting style and the values I have tried to exemplify and instill in my family and in my team.

Whether it's forces of Mother Nature or the cycles of the academic year, renewal and promise are in the air, bringing with them new energy and restoring our balance for a new beginning.

Coach P hugging Jasmine Thomas during postgame press conference on March 7, 2010, following the 2010 ACC Championship win in Greensboro, North Carolina.
Source: Orin A. Day (DWHoops.com)

Coach P's daughter, Maddie, playing summer basketball with the New England Crusaders during July 2010. During the fall of 2012, Maddie will begin her college education at Miami University in Oxford, Ohio where she will also be on the women's basketball team.

Source: Personal Collection

ACKNOWLEDGMENTS

As a wise man once said to me, "Writing is harder than coaching." And he was absolutely right. There are so many special people to thank for making this project possible.

Rob Rains is a terrific person with a wonderful ability to write so clearly and with great detail. Dan Ambrosio and Christine Moore were invaluable with their expertise, humor, and focus throughout . . . not to mention their patience with every question.

Eleanor Cooper's wisdom and terrific sister-in-law advice, not to mention her incredible editing and writing skills, are so appreciated. Thank you, Ele, for making me better and teaching me about your craft.

A special thank you to Joe Alleva for giving me the opportunity to coach at Duke. Thank you to Kevin White, as well, for allowing me, my family, and teams to thrive under your clear and thoughtful leadership.

Thank you to Mike Krzyzewski for your support and clear messages and lessons regarding all things Duke. It has been an unbelievable five years so far. You and your program have challenged me to become better and stronger in all ways.

Thank you to an amazing staff, who all gave me opinions and thoughts throughout this process. Al, Bobby, Kate, Lauren, Candice, Joy, and Sarah, you are so appreciated.

A special and most sincere thank you is needed for Kevin Lehman, who truly stayed by my side with every detail from start to finish. Your work ethic and commitment to me and Duke is so appreciated.

To all the players I have been most fortunate to coach, thank you for believing in dreaming big and pursuing championships in all that we do.

To my family and amazing parents, thank you for helping create the stories that were so enjoyable to share in this book. Special thanks to my mom and sister for always being there for me.

And finally, how do you thank a man who has been with you every step of the way for more than 20 years? John is truly the most unique thinker and friend I could ever hope to share life with . . . it has been, and continues to be, a great life.

UNIVERSITY OF MAINE AND MICHIGAN STATE UNIVERSITY

Through the years I have been fortunate to work with so many talented players and staff members. The following people, at the University of Maine and Michigan State, paved the way for me and my family. You all are so appreciated for making our lives fuller, richer, more humorous, and filled with incredible memories. Those of you who were part of that amazing 2005 run to the National Championship game, please remember the connectedness, resilience, and commitment to each other that we shared. Those moments reflect such chemistry and dedication from so many.

Sam AcMoody, Trena Anderson, Lauren Aitch, Myisha Bannister, Jody Benner, Darren Bennett, Cindy Blodgett, Lamar Boutwell, Lindsay Bowen, Kelly Bowman, Heather Briggs, Syreeta Bromfield, Jessie Bruyere, Cyndi Buetow, Caroline Nixon Burgess, Niya Butts, Jennifer Callier, Sandi Carver, Jamie Cassidy, Vance Catlin, Andrea Clark, Katie Clark, Pam Cruz, Becky Cummings, Klara Danes, Courtney Davidson, Nikki Davis, Carla Debro, Alyssa DeHaan, Gabrielle Deshong, Seana Dionne, Danielle Doneth, Marian Dressler, Maggie Dwyer, Cortnee Ellis, Heather Ernst, Catherine Gallant, Ellen Geraghty, AnnMarie Gilbert, Erin Grealy, Janel Grimm-Burgess, Carolyn Gross, Christy Grover, Tracy Guerrotte, Stephanie Guidi, Joe Guistina, Brad Gust, Laura Hall, Rene Haynes, Kristin Haynie, Katie Abrahamson Henderson, Melissa Heon, Chelsea Hopkins, Anna James, Aisha Jefferson, LouAnne Jefferson, Donita Johnson, Joy Johnson, LaKendra Johnson, Mia Johnson, Kalisha Keane, Nate Lake, Kim Lazar, Felisha Legette-Jack, Kizzy Lopez,

Victoria Lucas-Perry, Chantal Macream, Katrina Grantham Masters, Kristen McCormick, Patrice McKinney, Liz Shimek Moeggenberg, Eva Moldre, Becky Olsen, Megan Osmer, Julie Pagel-Dombroski, Andrea Pardilla, Anne Peck, Mandy Piechowski, Ben Phlegar, Jenny Poff, Stacy Porrini, Christie Pung, Semeka Randall, Maria Recker, Vnemina Reese-Cooper, Trisha Ripton, Paul Rivers, Joe Roberts, Kelli Roehrig, Stacia Rustad, Abby Salscheider-Alt, Lori Schulze, Ed Scott, Margaret Selasky, Erin Skelley-Smith, Melanie Small, Lacey Stone, Chrissy Strong, Kelly Stubbs, Rita Sullivan, Brittany Thomas, Martha Tinklova, Katti Towle, Amy Vachon, Julie Veilleux, Cetera Washington, Sherrie Weeks, Julee Woolston-Burgess, Alisa Wulff.

DUKE UNIVERSITY

I reserve a special thank you for all the players and staff who have done and continue to do so much at Duke. This group is a wonderful mix of Duke old and new. Our experiences together reflect a special and unique bond of mastering transitions within a top-level program and remaining committed and motivated to grow the unique and very high standard Duke commands. Pursuing championships daily, while challenging ourselves to do more, has been a wonderfully fulfilling and rewarding pursuit for the past four years. It seems that we all are more motivated than ever. Thank you for all that you do.

Missy Anderson, Chante Black, Al Brown, Lindy Brown, Joy Cheek, Karima Christmas, Carrem Gay, Chelsea Gray, Amber Henson, Candice Jackson, Keturah Jackson, Richa Jackson, Ka'lia Johnson, Alexis Jones, Kevin Lehman, Trica Liston, Summer McKeehan, Brittany Mitch, Bridgette Mitchell, Sierra Moore, Shannon Perry, Haley Peters, Lauren Rice, Alexis Rogers, Kathleen Scheer, Shay Selby, Kate Senger, Wanisha Smith, Sarah Smoak, Bobby Sorrell, Trisha Stafford-Odom, Jasmine Thomas, Krystal Thomas, Allison Vernerey, Abby Waner, Emily Waner, Chloé Wells, Elizabeth Williams, Samantha Williams.

INDEX

Acupuncture/acupuncturist, 113, 114, 120

Advice, willingness to accept, 12, 83, 84, 126

Alleva, Joe, 13, 183

Angelou, Maya, 214, 216

Assistant coaches
  at Duke, 176, 177, 215
  graduate assistant coaching position at Auburn, 54–56, 60–65, 69, 70, 154
  at Michigan State, 176, 177
  role of, 177
  transition to head coach, 71, 77
  at University of Maine, 76, 113

Auburn
  choosing over Vanderbilt, 54–56, 60
  full-time assistant coach position, 65, 69–71
  graduate assistant coaching position at, 54–56, 60–65, 69, 70, 154
  MBA, earning, 65

Automobile accident, 2, 67–69

Bagley, Stan, 124

Bird, Larry, 34, 141

Blair, Gary, 172

Blodgett, Cindy, 79, 84–86, 89, 98, 100, 102–104, 108, 109

Boeheim, Jim, 189

Boston University, 80

Boutwell, Lamar, 89

Bowen, Lindsay, 137, 151, 153

Bowman, Kelly, 111

Brown, Al, 154, 177

Browne, Anucha, 40, 44, 45

Buyout clause in contract with Michigan State, 10, 12, 168–170

Callan, Carol, 164, 165

Career goals
  after college, 47, 52
  female coaches, 5
  head coach position, 70
  and marriage, 69
  support network, importance of, 83, 84
  support of husband, 67, 69

Carolyn (McCallie's sister), 172, 173

Carver, Sandi, 104, 109

Cassidy, Jamie, 104, 111

Change
  and clarity, 53, 54
  and growth, 191
  and leadership, 133, 176
  new coaches, 42, 43, 131,
    132, 178
  positive effect of, 53, 54, 133
  power to change and effect of
    choices, 19, 133
  in priorities, 108, 109
  readiness for, 12
  and replaceability of people,
    42, 43
Charles, Lorenzo, 34
Cheek, Joy, 215
Children. *See also* McCallie, John
    Wyatt (Jack); McCallie,
    Maddie
  choice in playing sports, 29, 30
  empowerment, 183
  motivation, 26, 27, 30, 31, 37
  parents as support versus coach,
    30, 31
  planning for, 88
  and quality coaching, 31, 32
  trusting, 183
  and work/life balance, 5, 6,
    86–88, 96–98, 119, 124
Choice Not Chance
  elements of, 18
  philosophy, 18–21, 134, 143, 149
Christmas, Karima, 21, 210, 213
Ciampi, Joe, 54–56, 61–65, 68–71,
    77, 78, 154, 173
Clark, Andrea, 111
Clark, Katie, 111, 115

CNC (Choice Not Chance)
    Ballclub, 19, 20
Coach K. *See* Krzyzewski, Mike
    (Coach K)
Coaches and coaching
  accountability and responsibility,
    78, 81–83, 162
  assistant coaches. *See* Assistant
    coaches
  challenges, dealing with, 208, 213
  change, 42, 43, 131, 132, 178
  communication with players,
    134, 136, 190, 191
  consequences, 193
  developing people and players, 64
  empowering others, 74, 76, 192
  female coaches, 5
  games, 75, 76
  hard work, rewarding, 192–194
  humility, 82
  inspiring, 192
  loyalty, expressing through
    actions, 62
  making sense of coaching, 63–65
  mentors, learning from, 77, 78,
    83, 84, 162, 175
  mistakes, learning from, 12, 62,
    63, 77–83, 193
  motivating players, 20, 74, 76,
    129, 130, 133, 134
  nonperformers, dealing with, 194
  passion for, 63, 177
  philosophy, 74, 75
  practice, 75
  process-driven, 75–77, 91,
    194, 216

recruiting, 198–201

relationships with players, 149, 190–193

responsibility for players, 200

seniors, treatment of, 193

summer camps, 201

teaching, 192, 208

team effort, 161

transition from assistant to head coach, 77

transition from player to coach, 62, 84

and work/life balance, 70

Collateral damage, 11

Commitment, 43, 44, 60, 61, 70

Communication

and conflict, 134

importance of, 136

in marriage, 69

with players, 134, 136, 190, 191

technology, impact of, 56

Competitive cauldron, 208

Conflict

and clarity, 45, 64

managing, 133–137

Contracts

buyout clause in contract with Michigan State, 10, 12, 168–170

reading and understanding, importance of, 169, 170

Cross-training, 30

Cutcliffe, David, 184

Decision making, 20, 182. *See also* Choice Not Chance

young adults, 20

Discipline, importance of, 27

Dorrance, Anson, 208

Driver's license test, 184, 185

Duke University

academic standards, 190, 198, 199

assistants at, 176, 177, 215

athletic director, 183, 184

coaching position offer (2007), 170, 171

connection with, 175

decision to leave Michigan State, 10, 11, 171

family adjustment to move, 182, 183

first year of coaching at (2007-2008), 178–182

fourth year of coaching at (2010-2011), 208–211

head coach position opening (1992), 70, 71

high school recruiting of Palombo (McCallie), 32, 33, 36, 175

initial meeting with Coach K, 13–15. *See also* Krzyzewski, Mike (Coach K)

mentors and role models at, 175

NCAA Tournament (2009, versus Michigan State), 4, 182, 195, 196

NCAA Tournament (2009)

versus Austin Peay, 195

versus Michigan State), 195, 196

NCAA Tournament (2010)

versus Baylor, 203, 204

Duke University (*continued*)
  versus Hampton, 203
  versus LSU, 203
  versus San Diego State, 203
  NCAA Tournament (2011), 211
  players, relationship with,
    190–193
  recruiting players, 198–201
  rivalries, 199, 210
  second year of coaching at
    (2008-2009), 190–192,
    194, 195
  third year of coaching at
    (2009-2010), 202, 203
  transition period, 176–178,
    182, 190
  and USA national team coaching
    position (2007), 174, 175
  "walk the dog" program, 130
  weight training, 178

Early life of Joanne P. McCallie
  basketball, 26–29, 31–36
  childhood, 24, 25
  college choice, 36
  college recruiting, 34–36, 45, 46
  first job after college, 52, 53
  high school years, 27–36, 45, 46
  international travel, 33, 34
  motivation, finding, 26, 27, 37
  move to Florida, 24, 25
  Northwestern, visit to, 36
  Parade magazine High School All-
    America team, 37
  parents, 24–26, 28–32, 35–37
  role models, 27–29, 31, 32

  small town life, benefits of, 26
  sports, 24, 26, 27, 29, 30
Empowerment
  children, 183
  role of coach, 74, 76, 192
Entitlement, 177, 192, 201
Erickson, Connie, 40
Ernst, Heather, 118

Family life. *See also* Work/life
    balance; individual family
    members
  marriage, 214, 215
  and moving, impact of, 3,
    4, 182
  support of husband, 67, 69, 88
  values, 6, 216
Fear of being wrong, lack of, 12,
    62, 63
Florida State, 99, 202
Focus
  and Choice Not Chance
    philosophy, 18, 19
  importance of, 61, 141
  and nervous energy, 135, 136
  on "next play," 163, 164
Friendships, 29, 42, 83, 84,
    140, 189

Garland, Mike, 125
Gender bias, 81, 95
Giannini, John, 96
Graduate assistant coaching position
    at Auburn, 54–56, 60–65, 69,
    70, 154
Graffam, Allen, 27

Granholm, Jennifer, 154
Gregory, Brian, 125
Griner, Britney, 203
Guerrette, Tracy, 116
Gunter, Sue, 102

Haynes, Rene, 153
Haynie, Kristin, 128, 129, 137,
    152, 154
Henson, Amber, 214
Heon, Melissa, 118
Humor, healing power of, 174
Hunt, Walter, 89

"If it's meant to be, it's up to me,"
    18, 19. *See also* Focus
Izzo, Tom
  lessons learned from, 13,
    125–127
  reaction to McCallie's decision to
    leave Michigan State, 172
  reconciliation with, 172, 173
  role of in recruiting McCallie
    from Maine, 115
  success as men's coach at
    Michigan State, 124, 125
  support from, 126, 127, 156

Jackson, Candice, 148, 149, 215
Jackson, Keturah, 203, 204
Jackson, Larry, 148, 149
Jacobson, George, 84
Jenka, Ed, 79
Johnson, Ka'lia, 214
Johnson, Magic, 140, 141
Joranko, Tim, 47, 48, 52–54, 140

Keeling, Rudy, 96
Kibo (dog), 130, 144
King, Angus, 99
King, Owen, 85
King, Stephen, 85, 86
King, Tabitha, 85, 86
Knight, Bobby, 194
Koerber, Fred, 27, 28, 32
Krause, Barb, 32, 33
Krzyzewski, Mike (Coach K)
  friendship with Jim
    Valvano, 189
  initial meeting with, 13–15
  lessons learned from, 163, 164,
    175, 179–181
  support from, 188, 189

Leadership
  and change, 133, 176
  communication, 136, 191. *See
    also* Communication
  confidence, 182
  and conflicts between team
    members, 136, 137
  decision making, 182
  in difficult times, 174, 181
  inspiration, 192
  leading by example, 161
  loneliness, 5
  motivating others, 129, 130
  nonperformers, dealing
    with, 194
  and personal life, 150
  philosophy, sharing, 74, 75
  responsibility and accountability,
    78, 82, 162

Leadership (*continued*)
  role of leaders, 161, 162
  and trust, 74, 75, 130, 131,
    180, 181
Lee, Phil, 54, 55
Leonard, Debbie, 70, 71
Long Beach State University, 44,
    94–96, 99
Lucas-Perry, Victoria, 155
Lynch, Annette, 41, 42

Maine. *See* University of Maine
Mary Margaret ("Mother
    Nature" acupuncturist), 113,
    114, 120
Mason, Ron, 155, 168, 171
McCallie, John (husband)
  age difference, 66
  and career goals, 69
  child care responsibilities, 88
  and decision to leave Michigan,
    10, 11
  first date, 65, 66
  marriage to, 69
  meeting, 65, 66
  Mount Kilimanjaro climb, 144
  move to North Carolina,
    responsibility for, 174
  parents' reaction to, 66
  purchase of house in
    Michigan, 124
  support from, 67, 69, 88
  values, sharing, 67
McCallie, John Wyatt (Jack)
  birth of, 118, 119
  pregnancy, 115–117, 119

school, 214, 216
  sports, support of parents in, 31
  and work/life balance, 119, 124
McCallie, Maddie
  birth of, 86, 87
  college plans, 214, 217
  father/daughter relationship, 88
  high school, 1, 182, 183, 216
  letter to, 1–7
  and move to North Carolina, 3,
    4, 174, 175, 182, 183, 185
  reaction to Duke loss at Michigan
    State, 4, 196
  sports, support of parents in, 30, 31
  straying incident, 101, 102
  and work/life balance, 86–88,
    96–98
McCallie, T. Hook, 155
McCormick, Kristen, 111
Media, dealing with, 82
Melanoma diagnosis and surgery, 2,
    187, 188
Mentors, learning from, 77, 78, 83,
    84, 162, 175
Michigan State
  arrival at, 124–126
  assistants at, 176, 177
  buyout clause in contract, 10, 12,
    168–170
  coaching position, acceptance
    of, 118
  coaching position, initial contact
    about, 114, 115
  conflict, managing, 133–137
  contract negotiations, 10,
    169–171

contract renewal after fifth
  season, 156
decision to accept coaching
  position at, 117, 118
decision to leave Michigan State
  for Duke, 10, 11, 14, 15,
  170–172
doubts about remaining at, 11,
  165, 168, 169
and family life in Michigan, 3, 4
fifth season of coaching at
  (2004-2005), 143, 144,
  148–156, 160–162, 170, 204
first season of coaching at
  (2000-2001), 76, 77, 132, 133
fourth season of coaching at
  (2003-2004), 142–144
goals for coaching at, 125
hiring process, 114, 115, 117
Izzo, Tom. See Izzo, Tom
men's basketball program,
  124, 125
motivating players, 129, 130,
  133, 134
NCAA Tournament (2003,
  versus Texas Christian
  University), 142
NCAA Tournament (2004)
versus Arizona, 144
versus Texas, 144
NCAA Tournament (2005)
versus Alcorn, 153
versus Baylor, 155, 156, 160,
  162, 204
versus Stanford, 153
versus Tennessee, 154, 155, 163
versus USC, 153
versus Vanderbilt, 153
NCAA Tournament (2006, versus
  Duke), 164
NCAA Tournament (2007)
versus Delaware, 168
versus Rutgers, 168, 169
NCAA Tournament (2009, versus
  Duke), 4, 182, 195, 196
player personalities, dealing with,
  136, 137
and process versus outcome
  philosophy, 76, 77. See also
  Process-driven coaching
reaction to announcement of
  coaching position at Duke,
  171, 172
Rosen, Lonny. See Rosen, Lonny
second season of coaching at
  (2001-2002), 135, 136, 140
seventh season of coaching at
  (2006-2007), 170
sixth season of coaching at
  (2005-2006), 163, 164
social time with team, 130
staff, rehiring, 131
third season of coaching at
  (2002-2003), 140–142, 202
transition period, 124, 125,
  130–134
WNIT tournament, 140
Miscarriage, 2, 108, 109
Mistakes, learning from, 12, 62, 63,
  77–83, 193
Motivation
  children, 26, 27, 30, 31, 37

Motivation (*continued*)
lack of, 20
and passion, 21
role of coach, 20, 74, 76, 129, 130, 133, 134

Neal, Stacy, 44
Negativity, avoiding, 6
Nervous energy, 135, 136
Next play, focus on, 163, 164
Nike, 78, 79, 85, 160, 189
"No scoreboard" mentality, 36, 37, 76, 77, 128, 209
Northwestern
basketball career at, 40–46
coach, departure of, 42, 43, 131
coaching position, consideration of, 112, 113
dating, 47, 48
education, quality of, 44, 45
first year at, 40, 41
friendships at, 42
high school recruiting visit, 36, 40
lessons learned at, 6, 46, 47
NCAA Tournament, 46
post-graduation plans, 46, 47, 52
support system, loss of, 41
women's basketball program, 41
women's sports, 41

O'Brien, Dave, 94
O'Connor, Rita, 29, 32
Oh, the Places You'll Go! (Seuss), 34

Opportunity
and Choice Not Chance philosophy, 18, 19
mistakes as opportunity to learn, 12, 62, 63, 77–83, 193

Palombo, Christina (McCallie's mother), 2, 3, 24, 35. *See also* Early life of Joanne P. McCallie
Palombo, Robert (McCallie's father), 3, 24. *See also* Early life of Joanne P. McCallie
Parade magazine High School All-America team, 37
Parents and parenting.
See also Children; Palombo, Christina (McCallie's mother); Palombo, Robert (McCallie's father)
guidance and leadership, 60, 61
involvement in children's lives, 26
and recruiting process, 200
role of, 31, 183
working mothers, 87, 88. *See also* "Superwoman" mentality
and youth sports, 29–32
Passion
for coaching, 63, 177
following one's passion, 54
lack of, 52, 53
and motivation, 20, 21, 26, 30
and work/life balance, 5, 6. *See also* Work/life balance
Person versus situation, understanding, 134, 149
Peters, Haley, 210

Pooler, Anne, 84

Poppovich, Gregg, 160

Power and control, 18–21

Priorities, reassessing, 148, 149

Process-driven coaching, 75–77, 91, 194, 216

Productivity, 20, 133, 161, 191–194, 202

Recruiting
  in 1980s, 34, 35
  college recruiting of Palombo (McCallie), 32–36, 45, 46, 175
  at Duke, 198–201
  and parents, 200
  role of coach, 198–201
  role of Izzo in recruiting McCallie from Maine, 115

Relationships
  breakups, 53
  building, 149, 150
  and change, 43
  coach-player, 149, 190–193
  and compromise, 12
  dating during college, 47, 48
  problems between players/ coworkers, 100
  and technology, 213
  and values, 42, 173

Rice, Lauren, 176

"Right thinking," 18, 19, 75, 134

Ripton, Trisha, 100

Rivers, Paul, 127

Roehrig, Kelli, 155

Rosen, Lonny, 128, 129, 176, 189

Rutgers, 168, 169, 179, 180, 184

Sabiston, Jim, 210

Sabiston, Susan, 210

Sanders, Anucha Brown. See Browne, Anucha

Shooting from the Outside (VanDerveer), 111

Silar, Jacki, 10, 11, 13, 172

Simon, Lou Anna, 169–172

Smith, Dean, 160, 161

Smith, John L., 144

Sorrell, Bobby, 176

Staying in the moment, 111, 192. *See also* Next play, focus on

Stiles, Jackie, 115

Stone, Lacey, 111

Success
  expectations, 132
  implications of, 94
  and need for continuous improvement, 95, 96

Summer camps, 20, 28, 29, 201

Summitt, Pat, 45, 154, 155

"Superwoman" mentality, 2, 87, 88, 96–98, 119. *See also* Work/life balance

Swimming, and African Americans, 211, 212

Taylor, Rick, 113

Teasley, Nikki, 117

Thomas, Jasmine, 21, 48, 202, 208–213, 216

Thomas, Krystal, 21, 210, 213

Tinklova, Martina, 111

Tirico, Mike, 172, 173

Title IX, 5, 29, 41, 87

Transferring schools, 43, 44
Tremitiere, Chantel, 63, 64
Trust
  children, 183
  and friendships, 42
  and leadership, 74, 75, 130, 131,
    180, 181

Underwood, Clarence, 114, 115,
    117, 119
University of Maine
  budget and program funding,
    94–96, 113
  coaching philosophy, 74, 75
  contract renewal, 113
  decision by Ripton not to play
    senior year, 100
  decision to leave for coaching
    position at Michigan State,
    117, 118
  documentary, impact of filming,
    103, 104
  eighth year of coaching at
    (1999-2000), 114–117
  fifth year of coaching at
    (1996-1997), 100–102
  first year of coaching at
    (1992-1993), 76, 77
  fourth year of coaching at
    (1995-1996), 96, 98
  head coach position at, 71
  men's coaches, relationship
    with, 96
  NCAA Tournament (1995, versus
    University of Connecticut),
    90, 91
  NCAA Tournament (1996, versus
    George Washington), 98
  NCAA Tournament (1997, versus
    LSU), 100–102
  NCAA Tournament (1998, versus
    North Carolina State), 104
  NCAA Tournament (1999)
    versus Old Dominion, 112
    versus Stanford, 110, 111
  NCAA Tournament (2000, versus
    North Carolina), 115–117
  Nike proposal, 78, 79, 85
  politicians, support of, 99
  scheduling error, 79–83
  second year of coaching at
    (1993-1994), 79–81, 86
  seventh year of coaching at
    (1998-1999), 110–112
  sixth year of coaching at
    (1997-1998), 102–104
  third year of coaching at
    (1994-1995), 84–86, 88–91
USA FIBA U20 team (2006,
  Mexico City), 24, 25, 164, 198
USA FIBA U21 team (Moscow,
  2007), 24, 25, 174, 175, 198

Vachon, Amy, 111
Values
  family, 6, 216
  integrating into work, 150
  and love, 67
  and relationships, 42, 173
Valvano, Jim (Jimmy V), 34, 189
Vanderbilt, choosing Auburn over,
  54–56, 60

VanDerveer, Tara, 111
Vevilleux, Julie, 118

"Walk the dog" program, 130
Warner, Pete, 99
Weight training, 132, 178, 211
Whining, 6, 43, 70
Whitaker, Chelsea, 162, 163
White, Kevin, 172, 183, 184
Wiggins, Candice, 153
Williams, Elizabeth, 214

Williams, Roy, 189, 190
Wittenberg, Derek, 34
Wooden, John, 160, 161
Work/life balance, 5, 6, 70, 86–88, 96–98, 119, 124, 201. *See also* "Superwoman" mentality
Working mothers, 87, 88. *See also* "Superwoman" mentality

Yow, Kay, 104, 166, 175, 176, 189